Praise for Robin Ryan and
What to Do with the Rest of Your Life

"Robin Ryan is the hottest career expert in America today. If you are looking to find a great paying job, she'll show you how."
—Susan Cowden, TV anchor, Northwest Cable News

"Hey, it's tough out there! So what a perfect time for a book that will help you land the job you want. Read this book, do what it recommends and you will not only survive, you will prosper."
—Vince Lombardi, author of *Coaching for Teamwork*

"I knew I needed to make a change. By following the techniques outlined in Robin Ryan's book I was able to see the opportunities and found the position that focused on what I truly love to do while providing a higher salary and a better life balance. Do you want to do what you truly love? Do you want to make more money? Do you want more time for family and friends? Well, I sure did and Robin Ryan showed me how, and that is why I think this is a must-read book!"
—Tracy White, director of human resources, Clark Nuber

"There's a reason why Robin Ryan is America's #1 career coach. She knows exactly what it takes to get hired."
—Mark Tranter, founder, America4Hire

"There's no greater challenge than finding a job you can really love. By following Robin Ryan's thorough, thoughtful advice, you'll greatly increase the odds of succeeding in your quest."
—Tony Lee, editor in chief, CareerJournal.com

"In my opinion, Robin Ryan has done a superb job in assisting others in their search for employment."
—Jay Brubaker, corporate recruiter

"I've worked with two big national outplacement firms, and we recommend Robin Ryan's proven strategies because they are the most successful."

—Suzanne Noonan, corporate outplacement counselor

"Robin Ryan knows exactly how to motivate you to create a better life with more money, success, and meaning. I enthusiastically recommend this book!"

—Cynthia Kersey, author of *Unstoppable*

"You'll find it's easy to be happier and more successful living a life of passion and extraordinary meaning once you've read this book."   —Victor Boschini, president, Illinois State University

Robin Ryan

A FIRESIDE BOOK Published by Simon & Schuster
New York London Toronto Sydney Singapore

WHAT TO DO WITH THE
Rest of Your Life

America's Top Career Coach
Shows You How to
Find or Create the Job
You'll Love

FIRESIDE
Rockefeller Center
1230 Avenue of the Americas
New York, NY 10020

Copyright © 2002 by Robin Ryan
All rights reserved,
including the right of reproduction
in whole or in part in any form.

FIRESIDE and colophon are registered trademarks
of Simon & Schuster, Inc.

For information regarding special discounts for bulk purchases,
please contact Simon & Schuster Special Sales at
1-800-456-6798 or business@simonandschuster.com

Designed by Bonni Leon-Berman

Manufactured in the United States of America

3   5   7   9   10   8   6   4

Library of Congress Cataloging-in-Publication Data
Ryan, Robin.
What to do with the rest of your life : America's top career coach shows
you how to find or create the job you'll love / Robin Ryan.
        p.   cm.
Includes bibliographical references.
1. Vocational guidance.   2. Career development.   3. Career changes.
4. Job hunting.   I. Title.
HF5381 .R7997   2002
650.14—dc21   2002066883

ISBN 0-7432-2450-7

To my husband, Steven, whose partnership enriches my life, and to my four-year-old son, Jack, who delights me daily and is the best blessing God ever gave me.

To my clients—nothing has been more rewarding than helping you find better jobs. May your lives prosper and your success continue to grow.

Acknowledgments

My mission has always been to help others find meaningful work, and many people have helped me in my pursuit of that goal. I owe a big thank-you to all the top executives who took time from their hectic schedules to complete my survey for this book. I'm particularly appreciative of the efforts made by CEO Debbie Coleman, who generously offered terrific insights into how top managers think and build multimillion-dollar businesses and brought me into her world to meet other women CEOs. I also thank Rochester Institute of Technology president Al Simone, who provided key assistance in recruiting other executives to participate in the top executive survey. Jim Medzegian's help was incredibly valuable—first in creating the survey, then in securing other executives to complete it.

Additionally, I am thankful to all of my clients who shared their stories so you could learn from their experiences. They are and always will be my reason for working.

Many experts made time for me and provided resources and referrals. I thank them all, but I must send a special word of gratitude to Azriela Jaffe, Joan Stewart, Diana Mandell, Paulette Ensign, and Sandy Dehan.

Sarah Lopez Williams has always been an insightful supporter of my career and proved to be a great friend and resource when she connected me with Paysha Stockton. Paysha was a godsend in helping me to better organize this book and improve it while typing it, too. Paysha, this book will help more people because of all your efforts. Thank you.

Janet Nelson skillfully translated many of my written pages into typed words, and I value her contributions.

Patty Lowe is by far the best nanny on the planet. For all of her love and the attentive care she gives to my son and our whole family—I offer a thank-you from the bottom of my heart. This book could never have been written without you and all you do for us, Patty.

Caroline Sutton encouraged me and gave me creative freedom to develop this book my way. She offered valuable insight that shaped the end result in the most positive of ways. She's been a terrific editor to work with, and I appreciate her efforts and support.

My mother, Jo Christiano, is and always has been a very devoted and loving mom and a key supporter who keeps me going in good times and in bad.

My work was most dramatically influenced four years ago when my son, Jack Michael Ryan, was born. He and my husband, Steven, taught me the true meaning and value of having and being a family. It is through loving them and being loved by them that I am a better person, mother, and career counselor.

Contents

Contents

Getting the Most from This Book

You have to expect things of yourself before
you can do them.
—MICHAEL JORDAN, BASKETBALL SUPERSTAR

You are probably wondering if this book can help you. The answer is, absolutely. If you are contemplating a change, I've provided this guide to make it much easier for you. I've worked with thousands of clients during my years as a career coach and have seen them experience so many circumstances or reasons for wanting something better. They, and even I, have been in the boat you're in, but with one obvious difference—the results. My clients ended up with careers they loved and were well paid to perform.

I wrote this book to team up with you as your career coach, to help guide you to the same positive, successful results. I've divided this book into three parts. Part 1 "Figuring It Out," is designed to help you evaluate your career choices and options and the quality-of-life issues we all face. You define your skills and ideal job. It will aid you in determining if you should stay, move on, press for a promotion, open a business, close your business and become an employee again, relocate, and how to better blend your career and family life. It includes strategies and help in prioritizing that will assist you in your decision-making process.

Part 2, "Moving On," covers the steps you'll need to take to land a new job or begin a new business. Emphasis is placed on achieving your salary goals as well as on finding a position that allows you (and your family) to have a life. It also outlines the practical steps and sacrifices needed to open and run a business, with special advice and insights from successful business owners and CEOs to guide your success.

Part 3, "Staying Put," is designed to help those who want to get promoted or land a raise within their current company. This section also covers proven strategies and marketing techniques for those who already own a business but want to reignite their passion and take their business to higher and more profitable levels. Again, top executives and successful CEOs and business owners surveyed for this book provide insight and guidance for reaching and even exceeding your goals.

You'll learn from inspiring client stories and noted experts, plus gain valuable insight from the CEO/top executive survey conducted specifically for this book. Proven strategies and techniques are clearly outlined and easy to follow and apply. I've included career trends that are reshaping the workplace and the strategies you'll need to effectively market yourself today, tomorrow, and in the years to come.

Let's get started. All the motivation and tools you need are in these pages. Together, we *can* and *will* positively change your life.

> Remember, the very best way to predict your future is to create it!
>
> —ROBIN RYAN

PART 1
Figuring It Out

When I was a child, my mother said to me,
"If you become a soldier, you'll be a general.
If you become a monk, you'll end up as the
Pope." Instead, I became a painter, and
wound up as Picasso.

—PABLO PICASSO

CHAPTER 1

Define Your Passion

I've always believed that any person with a
little ability, a little guts, some persistence, and
some determination could achieve whatever
he or she could dream.

—RR

Are you ready to move on? Make a change?

You'll spend about eleven thousand days working over your lifetime, and I believe they should be rewarding and happy ones. This book's goal is to help you decide how you're going to spend your days—at what job, at what level, where you do it, and how it will affect your life and your family for all the weeks to come. It's not just a career book, though, because—contrary to public opinion—you cannot compartmentalize your life. You have only *one life*. Your career, your family, your hobbies, and your socializing are all parts of your life—the only life you have to live. So, as we work together, I'll refer to your life and how you'll blend your career goals with both your family and your financial needs.

The first thing to determine is *exactly* what you want. I've worked with many clients who have faced the decisions you face now and moved on to a better and more fulfilling situation.

Successful people love their work, excel at it, and find meaning and happiness performing it. You are about to investigate many potential options: something new, bigger, better, different, or part-time, or even something you create and own. You can ponder and explore a new field or industry, land a promotion, and perhaps even consider a new location. You might be burnt out or simply want a position that allows more flexibility and time to be with your children. Starting completely over at the bottom in a new career just isn't financially feasible for a lot of people whose lifestyle includes a house, two cars, kids, and so forth. But changing careers doesn't have to mean a big drop in pay, as you'll see in later chapters. We'll look at your income objectives and make that a part of your career goals. Maybe all you need to do is clearly sell the skills and talents you already possess. You may need training or more specialty courses or even a degree to make your move. We'll investigate it all and set a plan of action in motion. If a move up is in your future, then hold tight, for included in this book is a new CEO/top executive survey on exactly *how* to get promoted and even reach the top if that's your goal.

Why Change?

For some people, that question has a simple answer—they just want to. It's a quality-of-life issue. They might be bored and want to tackle a new challenge. For others, the process is more agonizing. It seems job-hopping is really easy only for a relative few! Most people are willing to tolerate impossible situations and schedules, bosses who are demanding to the point of being ridiculous, and the feeling that the company owns them. Financially they feel they have no choice but to stay in their present job and at their present salary level, even if they dream every day of doing something else. Sometimes it's a sinking feeling of anxiety deep in your gut that tells you something is wrong. No matter how much wishing, hoping, or denial you engage in—you just know your job doesn't work anymore. Sooner or later, most of us face a moment of truth in our careers. Yet from these despairing times often come terrific new roads to follow. Sometimes change is forced on you. Losing your job is one of the most stressful things you'll ever live through, and it can be quite painful, too. No matter how many people have survived it and prospered, being fired is still an awful experience. Companies can call it something else—a layoff or downsizing, for instance—but the bottom line is that you don't have a job anymore. How you interpret this job loss—whether you think, "My world is ending," or, "Let's get something better"—can make all the difference in the world. I've seen many clients use layoffs and terminations as springboards into careers that are more rewarding, more satisfying, and more lucrative. In fact, 77% of all laid-off workers found new positions earning 15% more than they did in their previous jobs, according to the California Department of Labor.

Your reason for contemplating a change may be simply that there's no challenge left in your job and you're bored. More than likely, you are living as if you could separate your work from your life. What a ridiculous myth that is. Your career is a part of your life, your identity, a part of who you are and how you feel. For example, if you woke up tomorrow and your boss said, "You're fired," that would definitely upset your whole life. The fact that your career and your life are intertwined is one thing we must acknowledge when we face life's great challenges, such as divorce, the death of a family member, a personal illness or sick relative, even a pregnancy. These situations can become long, emotional, and sometimes physically debilitating and so require perseverance—plus added coping mechanisms to manage your career.

Maybe you are a victim of job burnout. This condition of extreme job dissatisfaction is often the reason many teachers, lawyers, nurses, therapists, and others change careers. Any job can result in burnout if an employer demands superhuman effort to get the work done. Ask yourself these questions: Do I feel overextended, tired, used up, unable to recover? Am I doing just the bare minimum at my job? Am I sacrificing my home life for my job? Am I stuck in a dead-end job? Is my work meaningless and of little consequence? Do I feel isolated at work?

Berkeley professor Christina Maslasch, a pioneer researcher and author of *The Truth About Burnout,* said that no amount of self-improvement can fix job burnout since its source is indeed *where* you work. She concluded that only by changing your workplace can you save yourself. Dysfunctional workplaces come in all shapes and sizes—nonprofits, companies, schools, colleges, firms, practices—but remember, not every workplace is dysfunctional. When our situations get dismal, we tend to write off the entire work world. But the grass can and will be greener elsewhere. Maslasch's studies state that there are six key areas for a worker's happiness: a manageable workload, a sense of control, the opportunity for rewards, a feeling of community, faith in the fairness of the workplace, and shared values. Let these keys guide you as you assess your situation and make your career decisions.

Life circumstances could be forcing you to change. Divorce is a major reason both men and women change or start new careers. Illness, your own or that of a spouse or child, may force you out of a job to pursue something new. Having to care for a sick parent (twenty-two million working people do) may drive your need to relocate and find a better, easier, more flexible job.

There could be another reason you're reading this book. You may be a business owner who is realizing it's time to close your business. Situations change. So do businesses. Losing big clients, industry changes, major setbacks, getting a divorce, remarrying, or having a baby can all make you want to reevaluate whether you want to keep your business doors open. Advertising genius Bob Serantino, a recent client who had this experience, said: "My own business was flying, but my divorce and custody battle was eighteen months of sheer hell. It pretty much consumed me, and I ignored the business, just doing the work that came to me. My zest to prospect for new business was gone. I guess I was too depressed after the divorce war to rebuild. I knew the enormous effort required to build it back up, and closing shop and going to work for someone else seemed a brighter and easier alternative." It was. He remarried, became the marketing director of a major pharmaceutical company, maintained some flexibility, and made more money than he had earned on his own in the last two years. He was also able to cut about twenty hours off his work week, which was a significant reason to make the change in the first place.

One of my clients, Sandy, found after several years that she loved training but disliked the hard work of marketing and selling her services as a business owner. So she came to see me about closing her training business. We decided that a corporate job with paid benefits would be her best option—and it didn't take long for her to find one. She heard of a great position with a Fortune 500 company. We wrote her resumé and a persuasive cover letter and polished up her interview skills. A few weeks later, her training company ceased to exist—she's still a trainer for that big company today.

Your situation might be similar or different. If you feel depressed, as though you are in a sinking ship or floating in a life raft, becoming an employee again might be the right answer.

And, of course, there all those retirees who have created a whole new trend of people seeking a career change. "Retirement's not all it's cracked up to be," said former school secretary Jo Madison. "You get bored and need something to look forward to. The fun-in-the-sun plan of going south for the winter gets, well, dull. Playing shuffleboard and going to bingo isn't my idea of living at fifty-five. I want to do things that matter."

"Golf was all I ever dreamed about," said forty-eight-year-old Mike. "I knew all I'd do was golf once I quit the rat race. So when the pressure cooker got so overwhelming at my store manager job, I took the early retirement severance package. And

I golfed and golfed, but found that I eventually needed more. I started a whole new career in a completely different field, minus the stress I used to face daily, and I just love every second of it."

People Need a Sense of Purpose to Have Meaning in Their Lives

Diane MacDonald, a business lawyer, financial planner, college professor, and author of *Personal Finance: Tools for Decision Making* (1999, Southwestern Publishing), enlightens us as to another reason retirees are headed back to work. "Mandatory retirement is quickly becoming an archaic dinosaur. With many people now retiring at fifty-five or sixty, they can have twenty to thirty years of life left. Working will be a necessity. Social Security income might not be enough, even with retirement savings, to get by for the long life span people are living," she noted. "A big mistake *many* make in their financial planning is thinking their cost of living will decrease dramatically. Retirement is never as cheap as people expected. The reality is that most people need to make 80% of their working salary to afford their retired lifestyle."

You may not be a retiree—perhaps you're returning to work after you've been home raising kids. This is a big decision. You must work through the hard stuff, like thinking about shift times and child care arrangements, while silencing the thoughts that question, "Will *anyone* even hire me?" If you've been out of the workforce for an extended period of time, you wonder if the skills you possess are marketable today—perhaps your old position was too far in the past to be of value. Have you been out of the workforce too long? Do you need classes or training to allow you to return to a higher-level and better-paying job? What volunteer work have you done? Do you want part-time or full-time work? Should you go to a temporary agency? These questions and many other doubts may be going through your mind.

There is also another significant factor that motivates a great number of people to change careers. They desire a position in which they are better able to blend work and family. I know this was true for me after my son was born. I had to learn new ways to blend this new career—motherhood—with the career consulting I loved to do. Nothing changes your life like having children, and this is true for men and women.

Many people have jobs for which they have sacrificed or obtained a great deal of education and training. They've given up a lot to get to the top. They also face a reevaluation of goals once their children are born, and as they raise them the issue continues to pop up.

If you are a working parent, this book will offer you new ideas and real strategies for creating a better life with more time for yourself and your family. It will also cover strategic advice on how to get a raise or negotiate salary to be paid the most possible for the work you perform.

No matter what your circumstances, moving on and creating a good plan on what to do with the rest of your life is key. Alexandra Stoddard, author of *The Art of the Possible,* summed it up very well: "Work holds a powerful place in our lives. When we're good at what we do, we feel tremendous satisfaction and pleasure. It is in the process of doing the act of work itself that we feel most alive and vital."

The Hottest, Fastest-Growing Career Fields

I'm often asked about the best, newest, or hottest fields. People are shocked when I reply, "Who cares?" People expect that a national career expert should be able to recite this stuff off the top of her head. But the latest fad or hot job doesn't matter if it's not in a field of interest to you or doesn't involve doing something you like. "C++ programmer" might be the hottest job going—are you willing to go back and learn C++ programming so you can do math all day?

Trends are important when they affect the field you want to enter. Many people recognize that certain jobs are going away and thus look into what is developing. But don't put the cart before the horse. Determine your true passion, and then together we'll uncover the ideal job and determine your target position. From there, we'll go out and get it.

Our Identities and Our Careers

Some people *are* their job. Many of us get a sense of worth, recognition, respect, and power from our work and the positions we hold. This has been true for men for many years—their entire identities can be based in their job titles and the positions they hold. This fact became profoundly apparent after corporate America downsized former VPs, CFOs, managers, executives, and CEOs. These people suddenly found themselves heads of nothing. They lost their identities, and some lost themselves. Some restored their own sense of self-worth or value with new employment. Some improved their careers, but others never regained their former prestige. Many women have also experienced this, especially as they have risen to positions of control and power. Passion and identity are closely linked.

In the survey conducted for this book, our top executives shared freely about exactly what drives them. The most common theme that emerged was that they loved their work and all took great pride in what they do.

As you begin to explore your future, you must think through your own motivations. Success is knowing what matters to you uniquely and personally, then applying perseverance to grow and make good choices. Ask yourself what is necessary for you to feel worthwhile, fulfilled, and happy.

Lou Holtz, Notre Dame's legendary football coach, offered some insight: "There can't be anybody who is less talented than I am as an individual, but I have a philosophy for success. I think attitude is the most important thing in this world. Attitude is something you control. You were given a lot of wonderful powers. You have the power to think, to love, to create, to imagine, to plan. The greatest power you have is the power to choose. We have to remember that we are in charge of our own lives by the choices we make."

Think about and answer these questions: How do I define my professional identity? How do I feel about myself and my job, and how do I want others to see me? What's my attitude and commitment toward success? What feelings must I get from my job to make it feel worth doing? What motivates or drives me? Most important of all, what do I really want out of my life?

CHAPTER 2

Identify Your Best Skills, Values, and Interests

The hardest step to take is the first one.
Once you've taken it, the rest get easier.

—RR

A recent *USA Today* survey, conducted by the Gallup Organization, posed this question to adults: "Which would help you be more successful in life: knowing what your weaknesses are and attempting to improve them or knowing what your strengths are and attempting to build on them?" Of those who responded, 52% said knowing and improving weaknesses and 45% said knowing and building on strengths. What do you think? The best way to build a career, according to recent research, is to enhance your strengths. "Strengths" can be defined as those talents and skills you do well and that seem easy for you. Many top executives in our survey pointed out that not enough people play up and/or enhance their strengths. These are your natural talents, your innate aptitudes. For example, some people have a natural flair for color and decorating, others are great at organizing, some are good at designing or building, while others find writing easy. Your strengths make you unique. New workplace studies show that focusing on your weaknesses can often be a waste of energy. You're better off finding a job that uses your strengths and doesn't require you to invest enormous amounts of time and energy in areas you can delegate or that aren't essential to performing your job. One client I had, a manager, had weak budgeting skills. Try as she might, she just couldn't master the financial knowledge required to do her current job. She was eventually fired, which devastated her. After examining both her strengths and her weaknesses, she landed a new management position where she was only peripherally involved in the finances. There, she was able to advance and use her leadership skills in an executive director role that drew on her strengths—developing her organization, handling relations with city and state governmental agencies, and working with the media. Playing off her strengths, she's been enormously successful and has bounced back from being fired. She learned what she does best and what she's better off having someone else take care of.

This does not mean you should ignore everything you don't do well. You can and will benefit from learning new skills and enhancing weaker ones. For now, trust yourself and think about your innate, God-given talents—ones that are unique to you. Your skills are many, as you'll see when we begin the process of identifying and defining your passion. Whatever you do, do it to the best of your ability. Your future comes from focusing on your talents.

Finding your true passion starts with skills identification and noting your strengths. In my work with thousands of career counseling clients, I've discovered a simplified approach to uncovering passions and ideal jobs. My process consists of the several priority lists and assessments you are about to complete. In my experience, career satisfaction comes from incorporating three areas—your top skills, interests, and values—into your job, so let's evaluate yours.

Skills Identification

In their hiring practices, employers today are expanding from the old method of "find someone who fills the job description" to a broader concept. Large and small companies are seeking a skill set that includes the necessary technical expertise plus the ability to perform at a higher level of productivity and interact in a positive manner to get the work done. To provide keen insight into many aspects of career management, I enlisted the cooperation of seventy-eight top executives from various industries across the country to participate in a comprehensive survey. These CEOs, presidents, organizational directors, and administrators offered valuable advice that will be quoted throughout this book.

Our survey respondents were crystal clear about what matters most to them as a boss—**"results."** You must be highly productive and good at your job, no matter what position you hold. That's an easier goal, the top executives said, if you enjoy your work. Top executives seek workers who possess personal traits such as flexibility and the ability to adapt to change. They also evaluate the standards of quality and excellence reflected in your past work. Personal productivity is a new measuring stick to evaluate potential employees and their attitudes toward success.

One CEO said, "If you can't do your best, then why show up? You'll never succeed at something you don't like. The drive, extra sweat, and effort come from pursuing something you were meant to do—drawing on your natural abilities and putting your whole heart and soul into it. When you do that, your success is guaranteed."

We'll begin with the skills identification, which will help you assess the multiple talents you possess. Use these as a starting point and then create a complete and thorough list of *all* your skills and strengths. When finished, you'll be amazed by the number of skills you possess and can sell to an employer. To get you started, I've listed a few common job-related skills. This is a brief list—not comprehensive at all, as there are hundreds of skills workers can possess. So add your own to the list you'll now create.

SKILLS ASSESSMENT CHART

Adapt tools, machinery, and equipment
Advise others
Analyze data
Audit or balance financial information
Budget time, resources, or materials
Budget management
Calculate numerical data
Compile research data
Complete projects or tasks on schedule
COMPUTER SKILLS: Note all
Conceptualize ideas
Conduct statistical analysis
Conduct market research
Control costs
Construct or assemble things
Coordinate services
Create displays
Create advertising/marketing materials
Create graphs/charts
Critique or review others' work
Curriculum development

Demonstrate how to do things
Demonstrate strong interpersonal skills
Design buildings
Design flyers, brochures, booklets, etc.
Detail-oriented person
Detect problems or errors
Diagnose technical problems
Dispense medicines
Document records
Edit written material
Effective listening skills
Encourage productivity in others
Establish policy and/or procedures
Estimate space or cost requirements
Examine products or processes
Financial analysis
Financial planning
Follow-through on tasks
Fund-raising
Give presentations
Handle complaints
Hire people

Influence others
Install equipment
Interior design
Interview people
Instruct others
Interpret or translate a different
   language
Invent new products
Justify decisions
Lead a department
Lead an organization
Legal expertise
Make business deals
Manage people
Mentor others
Merchandising of product(s)
Multitask
Negotiate contracts
Operate equipment or machinery
Originate new ideas or
   procedures
Organize data or information
Organize people
Organize processes or systems
Organize programs
Perform labwork
Persuade others
Plan agendas
Plan events
Possess manual dexterity, eye-
   hand coordination
Problem solving
Productive—able to get things
   done
Produce films or videos

Program administration
Project management
Public speaking
Purchase products or services
Process improvement through
   more efficient or effective
   ways of performing a task or
   function
Promote products, services, or
   events
Quality assurance
Quality improvement
Rehabilitate others
Schedule others
Sell products or services
Set realistic objectives for self and
   others
Set up systems, services, or
   programs
Solve technical problems
Supervise construction projects
Supervise installations
Supervise staff
Team builder
Test others or objects
Treat ill people
Use multimedia equipment
Use sophisticated equipment,
   instruments
Use scientific/medical
   instruments
Verbal communications skills
Visionary
Write technical materials
Written communication skills

Note any additional specialty skills or industry knowledge you possess that may be marketable to employers or that you plan to acquire. Most of us will be lifelong learners, a key strategy to insuring job security. By continually learning new skills and improving your performance on the job, you can become and remain an invaluable member of the team.

Don't underestimate the importance of volunteer skills. Volunteers often disregard the value of their experiences. When I met Kristen, a mother of three kids, her first question was, "Do you think anyone would hire me? I've never worked a day in my life." One look at the resumé we created for her shows you how she spent her time—volunteering. She had achieved a lot, executing major fundraisers and large three-day conferences. Kristen acquired many valuable skills through her community activities, but until our career counseling session she didn't feel that her skills would have value to a potential employer because she hadn't been paid for her work. But that was far from the truth. Once we created her resumé, outlining all the event planning she had done, employers started to call. Kristen got several interviews and within a few weeks began a new job at a starting salary of just over $32,000.

Promotions often come about because you volunteered to learn something new. You may have acquired the opportunity at your job or from an outside organization. Many people get management experience from volunteering, then couple that experience with their current on-the-job skills to move on and up. I've asked many human resources managers about this. Maria, HR director for a large company, summed it up by saying, "We value many kinds of experience, and appreciate a person who has shown initiative through volunteer activities to obtain it. Women tend to disregard life skills—scheduling, budgeting, organizing events, and charity work. Planning a fundraiser and having two hundred people turn out is significant. It demonstrates organization and management leadership that's definitely needed in today's workplace."

In addition to making note of your community activities and volunteer work, plus skills you've acquired at them, also record all honors, awards, and positions of leadership (both volunteer and employer related) after your list of skills. Once you've completed all this, really look over your lists. Note your strengths and what you like to do most.

To help you make career decisions, we need to consolidate your skills and strengths. After you've created your master list, which should note dozens of skills, select your top ten skills and strengths. *Choose those you are proficient at and also enjoy using!* You may be great at something, but if you don't enjoy it then just eliminate it from your list.

Many times you can't achieve your goal without more training or education. This may mean some *big* sacrifices—working days and going to class at night or going to school full-time and living off loans or savings. People in their thirties and forties are returning to college in droves to get degrees and certifications and to learn new and different skills. Online educational opportunities allow more people flexibility. Dr. Michael Talbott, associate dean of telecommunications at Bellevue Community College, said, "The working world's need for lifelong learning is forcing people to continue their education, update skills, or learn entirely new ones. Technology has provided a very convenient way, using the Internet and computer to achieve this goal. Students use specialized software, email, chat, conduct discussion groups, and test—all online."

The key is to determine what skills and degrees employers say are needed to perform the job. The wonders of modern technology make updating skills a whole lot easier and more practical for the working person. If you elect to take online courses, be sure to stick with well-known, accredited universities. To learn about programs, contact your state universities and ask for "distance learning programs" for specific details on what's available. You can also look online—go to a search engine and type in "distance learning." Associations and business groups often offer some key training programs where one or two days can result in learning or improving upon a skill essential to moving on. Note any skills you want to work on or any training you plan to obtain to reach your goal.

Values Assessment

Values influence and shape your career decisions and are an important motivator in your career planning and job selection. Your priorities will change during your lifetime. What's important at age twenty-five—an impressive title and progressive company— might be replaced at age forty by a strong desire to spend more time with your family or to make more money. Let's determine exactly what matters most to you now. Review the following values and identify those most important to you. Feel free to add anything not covered in this list if it's a key factor for you.

VALUES ASSESSMENT

Acquiring new knowledge	Involvement in decision making
Autonomy in job	Leisure time
Beautiful work surroundings	Opportunity for advancement
Being around interesting people	Power and influence
Benefits	Public contact
Blending of family and career	Quality of product
Challenging work	Recognition
Clear rules and expectations	Regular 40-hour work week
Competition	Salary
Creativity	Security
Flexible work schedule	Status and prestige
Freedom from pressure and stress	Supervising others
Friendships at work	Taking risks
Helping others	Travel opportunities
Independence	Variety and change in work

| Working alone | Working with a team |
| Working from home | Working with details |

Values are our motivators. As you proceed to make career decisions, seek options that match your top values.

Blending Your Career with a Family

Your work life and family life are intertwined, each impacting the other. This is often a key motivation for change. Many desire something that will better allow them to find more time for their family. Others have demanding careers that require reviewing their priorities, looking at several options to improve on the job and be able to reduce some work hours. Then, of course, there are promotions—the bigger title and bigger job usually require more work hours. Consider how this will affect your family. Some promotions involve relocation. Ask yourself and your family: Do we all benefit, and is it worth it?

This blending of work and family must be decided based on your priorities and values. In a recent employment survey, 25% of all employee respondents replied that their top career issue was not salary or job security—no, balancing work and family was their top concern. The goal of this section is to help you, as a working parent, consider your values, options, and explore new ideas and strategies to make better overall decisions about combining these two parts of your life.

Many top executives in our survey warned us, saying, "Don't let your career ruin a great family life!" They were quite emphatic about that message. Yet so many working parents feel overwhelmed these days. A common theme I hear from my clients is that balancing work and family just keeps getting harder. People complain that there is never enough time, believing that balance is some mystical formula they just haven't gotten right.

The first and most important concept to acknowledge is that there is no formula for balancing work and family. There is no "balance," because "balance," defined by Webster's dictionary, means "state of equilibrium as to weight and amount," implying that there's a utopian midpoint you must seek out and achieve. This is a fallacy that most working parents grapple with. There is no balance of work and family—there is only a *blending of priorities*—your priorities! Only you can determine what's most important to you and then set your work and life priorities accordingly.

Careers give both men and women their identities, income, and sense of worth and power. Big careers take time—a great deal of time. Families also require time. You set the priorities, and you can adjust and change them as needed. So now let's identify your priorities, desires, and financial needs.

First determine your priorities. Write out, in black and white, what matters most. Everything comes with sacrifices. Terrific jobs, starting a company, relocating, promotions, going part-time, staying put in an unhappy work situation—all have a price tag. You may choose to decline some upward moves, electing to wait until the kids are older. If you do make the move, you need to determine how this will affect your kids and your spouse. You must also weigh your financial needs—the higher you go, the better the perks and pay. Some families want to have a parent at home, requiring the working parent to earn all the family income. The money has to come from somewhere—or, more exact, from someone who earns it. Be very honest with yourself as you review these questions. There are no "right" answers, no "wrong" answers, only what is true for you.

Take a moment to evaluate your financial picture. Note the dollars coming in and those going out, and prioritize how those dollars are best spent. Most people fail to take a clear look at their expenses. Examine fixed costs such as car and rent or mortgage payments over adjustable ones such as gifts, clothes, private schools, kids' activities, meals out, entertainment, and so on. Getting a true handle on your financial needs allows you to set goals and make better career and life choices.

Acknowledge one fact: You can't have it all. Each person has only twenty-four hours in any one day. You must set limits. The reality is that, over the last twenty years, both men and women have increased the number of hours they work at their full-time jobs. Women average forty-three hours of work per week, while men average fifty, and when you add on commute time it is clear that our work weeks are long. Sixty percent of all employees would like to work less, according to the Work and Family Institute.

The more successful you are, the harder it is to set limits. But you will burn out if you don't, and possibly risk losing your family. Consider both employers' demands (noting essential and excessive ones) and family obligations. You can't be all things to all people, so *make choices* and live by them.

Where you work makes a difference, so select supportive organizations to work for. You'll likely be more successful performing a job you enjoy at a flexible, family-friendly company. Flexibility is the key factor that allows most working parents to be productive and attentive at work. These flexible employers seem harder to find, but they are out there. You can find them and get hired by them, too.

None of us can be a superman or superwoman, and you'll save yourself a lot of grief by not trying to be. Not only must you set limits on the job, you'll need to do the same at home. Review all the household chores. Divide them into "must do," "could slack off on," and "don't need to do" categories. Try asking your spouse to pick up some of the load or, if you can afford it, hire someone to clean the house, mow the lawn, drive the kids to sports practice. Meeting other parents at your kids' school will allow you to join car pools, freeing up valuable time.

One other factor to review that contributes to hours spent away from the family is travel time. For those in a large city, reducing commute time is a big issue. One creative parent had the caregiver bring her daughter to her job—she then got to drive home in the car-pool lane with her little girl, cutting sixty minutes off her drive time. Another client, Ken, lived in a large city and averaged two hours a day commuting. He approached his boss about telecommuting and negotiated a schedule where he worked from home three days a week, reducing his commuting hours significantly.

Overnight business trips that take you away from home can be the hardest to cope with. Some working parents are honest with themselves about traveling and confess, "I need the excitement, the stimulation," or, "Frankly, I need the break." Others acquiesce and say, "That's the job," shrugging their shoulders as they leave the family behind. You must honestly assess your schedule and decide what's going to be best for you and those you love but leave behind. This is something you control—be realistic about how long you want to be away and the consequences of that decision. "Excessive travel" is often a key reason working parents change jobs.

Last, securing quality child care is a huge obstacle for working parents. Your work time is limited by day care or nanny hours or by your spouse's work schedule if you split shifts. Find reliable situations, set realistic goals and obligations, and have good backup plans for when you must work overtime, your child is sick, or your nanny quits. Once you've made some decisions on your family and work demands, you're ready to move on to make other career decisions you can more happily live with.

Perhaps you've wondered, "How do others do it?" How do the busiest people with the most demanding positions, the CEOs, top executives, and company presidents, manage? Two-thirds of our survey respondents said blending work and family is about priorities; 22% of our top executives wrote that "family first" is true for them.

Sue Carroll, owner of Western Insurance Managers, clearly made a different point that many other top executives echoed.

"Determine what is most important to you and whether those you love are willing to sacrifice anything for you to achieve it," she said. "If not, you probably need to rethink your strategy. Either find someone who is supportive of your decision, or else change your career goals."

Ellen Cagnassola, owner of sweetsoaps.com, voted emphatically for family first, saying, "Your kids do not look back on their childhoods and say, 'Gee, I wish you had bought me twelve Barbie dolls instead of only ten.' They remember walks, parties, friends, holidays, special moments alone. Make every one of them count . . . they are priceless and pass quickly."

It seems many executives were divided on this issue. Several CEOs and top executives clearly felt you cannot do both well. Many said, *"Choose!"* Several top women executives admitted to remaining childless in order to put all their energy into their careers. Most said they had no regrets, while others definitely felt they had sacrificed too much.

One woman CEO shared her story as a lesson to others. Although her own company, which she'd built, was a big success, she revealed that she had many regrets. "My nearly exclusive focus on the business was a major factor in destroying my marriage," she said.

A great many top executives had children, yet only a few had two high-power careers in their families, and those few had no children at all. Most top executives had a nonworking spouse, a husband or wife who took over the major role of caring for the kids and running the house. The obvious observation is that even the country's top executives don't have a formula for balance. Their key advice for blending work and family was to set priorities and live by them: Set boundaries, delegate, and take care of yourself and your family by making sure to build in personal time.

Our top executives offered several insights on how to accomplish this. "Think of creative ways of using your time. For example, instead of working every night until nine P.M., come home at six P.M. two nights a week and eleven P.M. two other nights per week. That way you will be home to put your kids in bed half of the time," suggested the owner of a multimillion-dollar organization. "Find a way to work while your kids are busy with school or sleeping so you aren't sacrificing their time." Many simply said, "Hire help."

Victor Boschini, president of Illinois State University, offered some sage advice. "Be realistic," he said. "Understand that nobody can do everything and keep all the balls balanced. Some 'things' must and will be sacrificed."

One woman company president wrote, "You can't have them [work and family] balanced. There is no such thing as Superwoman or Superman. I don't care what the world's common wisdom is today—you simply can't. You have to decide way ahead of time—long before you're destroying someone else with your decisions—which will hold more sway in your life. Can you have a fulfilling life and not just do one thing—family or work? Yes. Can you be great at both, which is what leading a balanced lifestyle implies? No. Could you teeter-totter both so that at one time work got 60% and your family 40%, then maybe family got 70% and work 30%? Sure. But you need to be realistic that you will not succeed with flying colors on both fronts."

Top executive Marcia Holland Risch had a great philosophy. She mentioned that she waited and raised her children before she began her quest for a top career, a path several women executives suggested.

Set Boundaries

It seems many top executives feel the need to draw clear lines in the sand. Pete DeBottis, a politician and top-level educator, said, "During any time off, away from your career, devote it exclusively to your family. Plan leisure time around the family, making them feel that they are as important to you as your career."

Donald Bressler, company president, said, "Build the family time commitment into your schedule and don't compromise on keeping those commitments. You wouldn't constantly break work commitments to your clients or staff, so give your family the same level of merit and respect."

Deborah Holland, a nonprofit executive director, warned, "A job will take as much as you give. Focus on results, and not hours at work. Don't allow people to get used to your burning the midnight oil or it will become a constant for you."

Exactly what is meant by boundaries? They're "the rules" you set regarding when you can't or won't work, the rules on family phone calls, interruptions, activities, and time together. The rules covering overtime, amount of travel, and hours worked. Your boundaries can even influence the company you choose to work for, since often you must live by *their* rules. Boundaries are needed to counter being always tied to your work and never really off the job 24/7, with pagers, cell phones, emails, and faxes making it too easy to do a little more work any time of the day or night.

Boundaries, as in priorities, are totally controlled and set by you. These are factors you *can* control, so you can arrange a life and career you want to live. So be honest with yourself—what do you want to limit, and what don't you? Be sure to think about the consequences, because it's up to you say, "Okay, here are my limits and here's how I'll do things differently."

Interests

What do you love? Your interests allow you to find pleasure in your work. If you really like computers, working at a software company lets you be with others who share your passion. If you love sports, you might find working for a sports team ideal even if you can't play for them. A producer position might be the perfect job for someone who loves television. It comes down to passion, and all that matters is what *you* find interesting.

Examine both personal and professional interests—let your mind roam and record everything that comes to mind—nutrition, music, travel, cooking, on-line auctions—anything you enjoy learning about, discussing, or doing. Create a list for yourself—try to write down forty or fifty things. Then prioritize and select your top five favorite interests. When deciding, consider this question: What interests me so much (for example, investing, health, news, management, and so forth) that I want to eat, think, and sleep it? Answer that and you've identified your key passion.

Creating Your Professional Profile and New Direction

"Look for something that you love doing and that you do well, that gives you joy and excitement every day. When you find something you love and something you do well, give it all your heart, all your soul, and all of your energy," advised General Colin Powell. To make career decisions, you must prioritize all your skills, interests, and values into a profile that will become the foundation for your career selection. The first step is to decide on your Top 10 Skills, Top 5 Interests, and Top 5 values, being sure to note the key objectives you have in blending your work and family.

Now review these lists. What jobs or careers come to mind when you consider all three components? Certain ones may pop into your head, but you can also brainstorm with other people to draw up a short list of possibilities. List these potential job titles. Then research each one to determine whether it would be suitable for you and note your research summary by each job title. Examine job duties, availability, potential future growth, salary range, and training requirements, and highlight whether or not you'll need more training to enter this field. List any

other factors that might influence your decision. Libraries are a
good source of career exploration reference materials, particularly books that define jobs, duties performed, outlooks, salaries,
and so on. Talk to people who perform the job to learn the true
duties and the pros, cons, pluses, and minuses to the work. Professional associations are also a solid resource for career descriptions—you can contact national and state associations and also
visit their websites to compile your summaries of potential careers. Create a career notebook for all the information you find;
add in the info you've uncovered so far. We'll reference it together as we proceed through the next two chapters and determine what your next career move should be.

CHAPTER 3

Determine Your Ideal Job and Workplace

The greater danger for most of us is not that
our aim is too high and we miss it, but that
it is too low and we reach it.

—MICHELANGELO

According to the U.S. Department of Labor, 46% of all workers leave jobs because they don't feel respected or appreciated. Your work environment plays a major role in your career happiness. You must therefore narrow down the type of organization you would like to work for, defining the specifics. Be honest with yourself about the types of environments that really charge you up and make you productive. This is the time to dream about where you want to work *every day*.

Let's systematically create an ideal company profile. First, determine the type of organization you want to work for. Is it small (500 or fewer employees), medium (501–5,000), large (5,001–10,000), very large (10,000–50,000), or giant (over 50,000)? Do you want your own company? Would you want to be part of a start-up that's not your own? Do you prefer a corporate environment, perhaps federal, state, or city government, or a nonprofit organization? What type of industry or field would you like to work in—high growth, stable, turnaround, prestigious, slower pace, or service? Do you want to work for an industry leader?

Now note the particular industries you really want to work in. Do you prefer business, broadcasting, construction, education, entertainment, healthcare, high tech, hospitality/tourism, manufacturing, nonprofit, publishing, retail, service, telecommunications, or another industry? Do you seek part-time, three-fourths-time or full-time work?

Then note the starting salary you want. Don't forget to consider benefits. They can enhance or detract from any job. For some, who receive medical and dental coverage through their spouse, benefits might be less important. For others, they are crucial. Define the five benefits you care most about. Rank them, with your top choice as number one and the next important as number two, until you've defined all five. Common benefits to consider are vacation (number of weeks), medical, dental, vision, retirement plan, profit sharing, stock options, bonus structure, commissions, maternity/paternity leave, flextime, business ownership, company car, expense account, on-site or paid day care, and life insurance.

Where you work also matters, so let's consider location. Last year, nearly two-thirds of all promotions requiring relocation were turned down, with employees citing "family considerations" as the reason for not moving. Consider where you will and won't live. Then list not more than three potential areas you are willing to move to. Note any and all opportunities in the area. Also set limits on how long a commute you are willing to make.

How much responsibility do you want? None? A great deal? Decide the exact level you want. For example, project manager with no supervision responsibility or VP, CEO, or department head with a lot.

Education and special training are vital components in pursuing a career, particularly a new one. Note all degrees, credentials, and special certifications you'll need to perform your desired job. List any training or academic degrees or programs you are currently participating in or planning to take.

Is Business Ownership for You?

Many of us fantasize about owning our own companies. Nearly one million new businesses are launched each year. In chapter 5, we will more thoroughly discuss business ownership as a career option, but I also wanted to mention it in this section as we work to identify your ideal job, career, or opportunity.

The positives of business ownership include being your own boss having power and control over all decisions, hard work, and long hours. All this benefits you personally instead of increasing profits for someone else. More income and growth potential; the ability to create excitement, variety, and challenge; and being in control of your own destiny are the advantages of this career choice.

These are the pluses, but there are some weighty considerations, too. I've talked with several business owners whose companies generated decent livings, as well as to CEO owners who gross millions of dollars, and every one of them confessed that their business was their life. "I worked all the time, totally obsessed with building my business," revealed Sunny Kobe Cook, founder of the giant national retailer Sleep Country USA. "When I lived in Texas, the Super Bowl was the major event happening in town, and I couldn't even have told you who was playing. Building my company was my life. There's much sacrifice needed to really make it big in today's competitive world. I worked incredibly hard and never gave up."

Many professionals—doctors, lawyers, consultants, and the like—say they work an enormous number of hours to establish their practice. Dr. Thomas Berstein found that establishing his medical practice consumed huge amounts of his time. "The first ten years were all spent building my practice, plus building referral resources and attending some educational and management classes. Patients don't just flood in the door the day you open. There are a million office and business procedures to learn, along with hiring and managing staff—and all this *after* you spend many hours seeing your patients. Any successful doctor will tell you that he works very hard, and most can't let up on the business, or it seems to start to just disappear and go elsewhere."

Opening and running a business is a major undertaking, but a career option you should consider. Many business owners are very happy people. Since it's a complex topic, chapter 5 is devoted to the decision-making process, and chapter 9 covers how to take your business to the next level.

Your Future

Goals—we all accomplish more when we have clearly defined objectives. Many people fail to realize that goals are simply dreams with deadlines. So now, really consider what your goals are. Think about what you truly want—short and long term. What are your family and financial goals? What personal achievements do you want to accomplish? To insure your professional future, you need to become a lifelong learner. List any and all skills, training, or degrees you want to acquire.

Now that you've completed these exercises, you have your essential skills and long-term game plan in mind. If you want to make it into the echelons of top management, good career planning and decision making are essential. Business ownership requires the same. So does changing fields, careers, industries, or jobs. The best thing about career planning is that you can always reevaluate and change your mind.

Define Your Ideal Job

This is a critical step in your decision-making process. Take your time defining the perfect job. You've already examined your background, skills, strengths, education, and goals and identified a specific job title. After reviewing the following sample, write a job description for yourself and define what would make a job ideal for you. Above all, the selection must express your inner passion—you must have a sincere desire to work and excel in this area. Note that this description should be written as if you *already* have this position.

Here's an example of one person's sample ideal job.

Title: Product Marketing Manager, high-tech company.

Description: My ideal company is medium in size, an emerging high-tech company where I'm the Product Marketing Manager. I'm heading up a new product marketing campaign and overseeing several employees in this process. The work is challenging, exciting, and high pressure, and the base salary is $80,000, with major bonuses and stock options tied to product and my personal success. I hold an MBA and rely on my computer skills, especially Excel, to determine brand penetration, forecasts, and profit margins. I've got terrific negotiation skills and have established key partnerships to aid us with product sales. I enjoy the challenge of launching new products—the design, planning, packaging, and roll-out process. My strengths lie in planning, budget management, promotion, creative ideas, coordination, problem solving, and interpersonal communication. I use these skills daily and truly love this job.

Now, write your own. To some people, working part-time is the ideal. Others want to travel and see the world. Still others want to run the show. Whatever goal you want to achieve is all that matters. Try to get clear on what you want and how it will work. Then write out your ideal job description.

Look Before You Leap

"Being paid well for something I would do for nothing—now that's lucky," said CNN talk show host Larry King. Luck usually comes from hard work, taking a few risks, and good decision making. Before you finalize your decisions, network and talk with successful people performing the job you think you want to do. Associations can also be very helpful. Identify the major association connected with your career field, visit its website, and even talk to the association's officers. If you want to open a business, try talking to a few successful owners who run companies similar to the one you want to start. This investigation is crucial to making sure the reality of living the job day to day matches your fantasy. Many lawyers wish they'd done this research *before* they went to law school, rather than finding out years later that they downright hate the "real" practice of law.

Putting It All Together

Don was a forty-three-year-old elementary school teacher who had grown dissatisfied with his job. His new interest involved computers. He took classes and taught himself all about technology, networks, and applying the Internet to the classroom. He thought life was perfect when he became the school district's "technology teacher" and began to develop online courses—very cutting-edge stuff. But when his administrative head changed, his job did, too. The funding was cut, projects were curtailed, and he faced a hard choice—head back to the regular classroom and teach fifth grade (taking a 20% pay cut) or leave.

We met and went over his situation. He still wanted to work in education but loved using his technology and curriculum development skills. He hoped to find innovative work that included both components. We worked on a goal—to find his ideal job—but I warned him it would be very difficult since few of these positions existed. We discussed potential companies and set goals, and he began networking. It took about three months before he landed his dream job—program manager for a university education department in charge of the elementary school online classes technology. Don tells me he's living his dream, is happier than ever before, and is making $75,000 a year—45% more than his elementary school teaching position.

Theresa was a successful dentist. Her income was substantial, and over the past twenty years she'd built a large, successful practice in Texas. She became active in her state association, eventually holding offices on various committees. She came to me to discuss a major career change she was thinking about—selling her practice and pursuing a career in association management. This was a huge decision, with a great deal of money at stake. But Theresa was worn out by the daily demands of insurance companies and financial pressures, and her job had become routine and boring. Then an injury made it hard to continue working, and she was no longer able to handle her previous fast pace. She'd loved the excitement and challenge of building her practice. In fact, her career profile noted variety and challenge as her two top values, along with exceptional skills in marketing, promotion, and organization. On paper the career transition looked like a great fit for her skills and interests. The reality of the change was a different story. She estimated that her $200,000 annual income would shrink to between $50,000 and $60,000. Plus, at fifty-one, she had no paid association experience, only volunteer work.

Together we worked on her resumé and polished her interviewing skills, as this transition would require a great deal of self-marketing. Next we created a list of networking resources, and she put her action plan in motion. I checked up on Theresa, and here's what she said about her results—she's now the executive director of the Virginia Dental Association: "I'm living proof that you can not only make a career transition from a job you were committed to for a lifetime, but you can do it and flourish, being happier and richer than you ever dreamed! Inner satisfaction and a passion for what you do make you rich in a way dollars and cents never can." Incidentally, she did take a pay cut, but far less than she thought—she still makes more than $100,000 per year.

I can recall hundreds of clients who changed their careers and moved on to something different and rewarding. Some were in their twenties, while many were in their thirties and forties. Even former clients in their fifties, sixties, and seventies made successful and rewarding career changes. One key to changing was using transferable skills. Theresa's years of volunteer experience laid the groundwork for the association management job she has today, at twice the salary she expected to make. She now gets paid to do all of the event planning, marketing, and membership development she did as a volunteer. These skills, coupled with her transferable business management skills, helped her achieve success at her new job. Don brought his program management experience, technology, and teaching background to a position slated for a Ph.D. candidate. He convinced the hiring committee that his transferable skills were more valuable (he has only a master's degree) and beat out numerous Ph.D. candidates.

As you review your profile and look for a new career path, ask yourself these questions:

- Which skills do I already possess that apply and transfer to this job?
- Will I really love working at all aspects of this job every day? If not, what limitations do I want to impose?
- What have I already accomplished that will allow me to earn a salary that's higher than entry level?
- What new skills must I obtain?

You'll be surprised when you realize that you really can pursue your passion, make the transition, and flourish, too. Later on in this book, I'll thoroughly discuss how to leverage your acquired and transferable skills into lucrative new and/or different positions.

At this point, you may feel you need more career guidance. It makes sense to consult a specialist to help you sort out your choices. Many times people say they want a career change, yet something stops them or causes them to fail. A good career counselor can clearly point out options you've overlooked. Their expertise is to analyze the world of work, then direct you toward new options as they assess your talents and skills. Many community colleges offer career counseling at no charge, but with limited or restricted services. If you'd like more assistance, here are some tips for finding a qualified career counselor:

- Ask for referrals from friends and from college career centers in your area.
- Obtain the counselor's marketing brochure, fees, and references or testimonials from past customers. Also, visit his or her website. Investigate the counselor's qualifications. Reputable counselors have a college degree (preferably a master's or higher) with a vocational counseling emphasis. Be sure to comparison-shop. Training and experience vary greatly.
- Use counselors with a well-established reputation. Avoid organizations that sell $5,000 (or higher) packages to help you find a job. Too many of these "packaged programs" use fear and intimidation as sales practices to get your money, but never live up to the promise that *they'll find you a job.* (Their small print usually has an escape clause that doesn't guarantee you anything.) A recent article in *Money* magazine identified these high-priced packages as the number one consumer rip-off in America.
- Select a counselor whose style is a good fit for you and your needs. Some counselors specialize in the self-analysis and ca-

reer exploration phase. Others may have more expertise in
the "job search" process—writing resumés and cover letters,
targeting companies, and helping prepare for interviews. You
may need to use two different people to aid you in achieving
your goals. Be sure their counseling style and coaching skills
match your personality and objectives.

- Consider vocational testing. Most community college career
counseling centers offer vocational testing to the general public. What many people expect is to be able to take a test and
get an answer. There is *no test* that you can take that tells you
in thirty minutes exactly what you should be. Typically, you
invest hundreds of dollars to take a battery of tests—the
Strong Campbell Interest Inventory and the Myers-Briggs
Type Indicator are commonly given. Both tests are simply a
piece of the puzzle, so be sure to seek testing that offers good
guidance and interpretation as part of the process. One excellent testing service is the Johnson O'Connor Research Foundation (800-355-3672), a nonprofit vocational testing service
with eleven offices nationwide.

If we have not achieved our early dreams, we must either
find new ones or see what we can salvage from the old.
There is clearly much left to be done, and whatever else
we are going to do, we had better get on with it.
—ROSALYNN CARTER, FIRST LADY

Career Killers to Avoid

"The worst career mistake is not taking the time to reflect on
what interests, motivates, and drives you. People float through
life as if it were boring, drudgery, or a nuisance—often complaining, yet never determining what would fulfill them. Once
someone really knows what they want and sets goals, the chal-

lenges to achieve 'it' (life balance, promotion, and so on) are exciting and much more fulfilling than just whining," noted Lauren Thomas, former nonprofit director of a professional society. Joe Sambataro, CEO, stated, "The worst career mistake people make is that they give up too soon."

Top executives sure have strong opinions on how people sabotage their own careers. This is an important section to read—digest it and implement changes if your goals involve being successful, no matter what level you select and aspire to. Here, direct from our CEO/top executive survey, are the biggest career killers you need to avoid.

- **Not producing results.** "You have to get things done," one Fortune 500 CEO wrote. Dozens commented in their surveys that one sure recipe for career failure is not producing results. If moving up is on your list, you must become good at what you do, follow through, and produce results. There's no other way to advance, according to our top executives.

- **Not working at a job you're passionate about.** Several CEOs mentioned this, stating you'll never be happy if you aren't excited, interested, and enjoying what you do. The vast majority noted that the true key to success is discovering your inner passion and then finding a way to work in that arena. Even if you can't do "it" (for example, play football), you can still be part of an industry or field you love, performing a job involved with it (such as coaching or marketing a sports team).

- **Seeking job security.** Sorry to tell you, but job security is dead! It does not exist inside companies—even government agencies have begun to downsize. Layoffs continue at an all-time high. "Today, job security is something you build for yourself," noted one CEO. "It exists inside you, in your own talents that will secure your next job." Labor studies estimate you'll change jobs twelve or more times during your working lifetime. Today your skills, talents, and abilities will insure you a lifetime of employment.

- **Thinking that money is everything.** "A common assumption, but one most people prove false when they find their ideal job," said the CEO of a prominent service company. "A reality I've observed for most people—executive or staff—is that they realize money means very little if you are truly unhappy." It's just not worth it to slave at a job you hate, no matter how much it pays. When you love your work, it doesn't even seem like work at all. Desiring job satisfaction is the number one reason people elect to find a new job.

- **Having a bad attitude.** "It kills even the most talented," said one top executive, who has observed many talented people rise and fall. The CEO of a $700 million organization blatantly stated: "You're going nowhere if your attitude sucks." That's pretty in-your-face, but it's true. Our CEOs noted, "Nothing moves you ahead faster than a great attitude." Operate from a you-can-do-it position. Attitudes are learned, and you can improve yours daily by working on it consciously and actively. Negative attitudes slow you down, but good ones are jet fuel, enhancing all you do.

- **Not believing in yourself.** General manager Michael Lowe wrote, "There are peaks and valleys in everyone's career path. Only you know if you are as good or bad as what's spoken about you. Your strengths might not fit in at a certain organization—kind of the round peg in a square hole. You can improve your entire life by admitting that, noting your strengths, and finding a new environment where your strengths are needed, wanted, and seen as assets."

- **Not solving problems.** Ann Salamone, a technology company CEO, was quick to point out: "Some people let a problem serve as an excuse for not accomplishing a goal. You'll never achieve productive results that lead to the *big* jobs if you don't master solving problems."

- **Fear of failing.** No one welcomes rejection, but fear may be all that stands between you and your dreams. Nagging doubts—*What if no one hires me? What if it's worse than this? What if I don't like the people? I won't get three weeks of vacation*—can hold you back. Business owner Victoria Kenward pointed out that it's a serious error to "wait for someone to hand you an opportunity, instead of making your own." In my experience, fear is really the culprit that prevents many people from finding better jobs or getting paid what they are truly worth.

- **Listening to others.** Your spouse, colleagues, parents, or friends don't always know what's best for you. One of my clients had a job that ensnared her in some terrible office politics. Her husband blamed her. "It's your fault," he said. "You can't get along with others. It's you, you're the problem." He only added to her pain and lowered her self-esteem. One day, after a bad confrontation at work, she decided she would quit. Her husband was not very supportive; he never wanted her to quit her job. She had listened to him for an entire year and endured the job. But when it got even worse, he still expected her to stay and just "live with it." It was a difficult time in her life. She worked hard to find a new job in an environment she could thrive in. It took six months, but today she's a customer service manager at a growing company that values her as an employee and has promoted her twice since she started. Only *you* are responsible for your career. Your friends and family members may have good intentions, but they don't walk in your shoes. Listen to yourself. Your dreams, your goals, are all that matter. Don't pay any attention to those well-meaning naysayers who warn you that you can't do it. Sunny Kobe Cook, founder of the national retail chain Sleep Country

USA, says, whenever she's asked how she got to be so successful, "I just assumed it was all possible, and that I could do it."
She did and so can you; the key is to believe in and trust
yourself to know what's best for you.

- **Waiting for employers to notice you.** Too many clients have
come to me frustrated over not receiving a promotion or
raise. They were doing a good job. In Debbie's case she had
finished her bachelor's degree, but no one had noticed. She
was waiting for her employer to notice her and give her a
raise or promotion. Waiting . . . waiting . . . waiting. Nothing
happened. She said, "I kept waiting for my boss to do something, waiting and expecting it should just *happen.*" After our
coaching sessions, Debbie changed her approach. She went to
personnel and got job descriptions for two other jobs in different departments, and we rewrote her resumé. She applied
and got called to come in for an interview. But ultimately
neither job appealed to her, so she kept at it. Within forty-five
days the right position came along. Her qualifications weren't
as strong as those of the two other candidates, but Debbie
persuaded the hiring manager—and she got the job. One
CEO said, "Stop waiting for your ship to come in; you've got
to be the one to make things happen. It all starts with what
you do and don't do."

- **Not having big enough goals.** "A key career stopper is setting
your goals too low or not being willing to put in the time it
takes to reach goals," noted CEO Randy Sheparo. "Believing
'I could never do that' or 'They'll never give me a raise'
means it probably won't happen." Many of us lack the confidence to boldly demand more, and it is almost always this lack
of self-confidence that prevents you from going after more—
a better job, raise, promotion, more time with family, and so
on. Yet we can all *act* as if we possess confidence. You can "act
as if" you merit a raise by outlining all your specific contribu-

tions to your employer. You can "act as if" you are the most ideal candidate the employer could hire by offering examples of past accomplishments. "Act and you shall achieve," noted a healthcare CEO. "Then, reevaluate and draw up even loftier goals—that's how you'll do more than you ever thought possible."

- **Trying to taking credit for things you didn't do or overstating your qualifications in the first place.** "You can't take credit for work you didn't do," advised one healthcare CEO. "In fact, a little humility and praising the whole team will get noticed faster than someone pulling rank and saying, 'I did it,' when the team (or someone on the team) really did." Today's workers want to be recognized and praised, so stealing their thunder will come back to haunt you, though you may get away with it in the short term. Many top executives noted that "bragging" and "accomplishing" are not the same thing. Exaggerating what you've done may get you in the door, but you may not stay there long. One sales manager said, "I've had many potential employees say, "I'm the best there is, and then you try them out and they prove they are far from great, and not even very good. That's the true test. I find the bragger usually hasn't got the skills to achieve real accomplishments, and that ends his or her career every time." Another president mentioned employees who give a lot of lip service about where they're going and what they want to do, but they have unrealistic expectations about *the real price* of reaching their goals. And that, she noted, resulted in their being unable or unwilling to work hard enough to achieve what they said they wanted.

- **Gossiping and playing office politics.** "I hate it when someone sabotages a superior to get ahead—that approach never works for long and really ends careers more than it makes them," one CEO said. "Gossiping is an immediate termination in my company," wrote another CEO, who's headed several large corporations. So many top executives noted that these two activities will undermine, cripple, and even destroy a career. "Some people pick the wrong battles to fight," another executive wisely noted. "When you get enmeshed in gossiping or office politics, you forget about the goals, mission, and getting the job done. It'll lead to a lack of outcomes—a career killer every time."

- **Not being flexible.** "I need you to be thinking strategically, to be flexible and adaptable to keep my business moving forward," said CEO Deidre Manning. "Flexibility is a key trait you've got to have to survive in the business world today, and many people lack it," noted another company president. The CEO at a major manufacturing company stated, "Trying to fight the reality within your organization will kill your promotion chances. Once changes are made, you need to roll with it—being too rigid and not being flexible is a huge mistake," he reported. Being flexible means learning new skills, trying to do things differently, and accepting change easily, noted most CEOs.

- **Burning bridges.** Victor Boschini, president of Illinois State University, offered this key insight: "I believe the biggest mistake people make in their careers is to burn bridges 'along the way.' Each profession may seem big—but I believe as you move up in your career you realize how 'small' each really is. It makes no sense to right every wrong you felt in a certain organization on the way out. This almost always comes back to haunt you."

- **Acting inappropriately.** In a frank discussion, several top executives mentioned that a rising star's career can often be derailed if his or her behavior gets out of line. Companies pay

Personal Career Management Guidelines

The following guidelines can be adapted and implemented as you navigate your career throughout your life.

- Develop a skill set—skills, talents, and experiences.
- Adopt attitudes that focus on personal excellence and quality.
- Be highly productive, organized, and efficient, and above all, produce results.
- Continuously acquire new skills.
- Emphasize customer service whether your customers are internal departments or external clients.
- Work well in a team.
- Focus your time and energy on success and successful pursuits.
- Reward yourself for both small and big jobs well done.
- Celebrate your victories.
- Put your personal goals and well-being ahead of company loyalty.
- Develop a reputation for integrity, fairness, and honesty.
- Continuously develop your professional network.
- Be involved in professional organizations/associations within your field.
- Remain current in your field.
- Do more than expected, and do it better than expected.
- Review your career every year and map out an annual plan.
- Do quality work in a productive manner.
- Perfect your communication skills.
- Acquire solid references attesting to past performance and excellence.
- Believe in yourself.
- Have a current, up-to-date resumé ready.
- Pay attention to potential career opportunities, and act upon them.
- Obtain the needed education and skills to land the jobs you want.

strict attention when someone is accused of sexual harassment or discrimination. Many said suggestive comments and
office affairs can end in terminations or stagnant careers. A
top executive with a major pharmaceutical company noted,
"I've seen alcohol destroy more careers. Social drinking with
clients can get out of control and eventually lead to a drinking problem. When it does, the career just goes downhill from
there."

- **Don't burn out.** "I've seen doctors, lawyers, teachers, counselors, and executives overextending themselves as a part of
the job. They are guaranteed to burn out. This always sets
people up to fail," noted a chairman of the board. "You must
set limits and balance your job by also having a life and making that matter, too."

Inability to make decisions, doing mediocre work, not producing results, or lack of drive and initiative can all jeopardize a
career. Not understanding the big picture, procrastination, even
thinking you know it all or that the rules don't apply to you can
be just as devastating to a career as overmanaging, whining, or
not being a team player. And it goes without saying that lack of
integrity, being dishonest, not keeping your word, or not fulfilling commitments are surefire career killers.

PART 2
Moving On

If you can *dream* it, you can *do* it.

—WALT DISNEY

CHAPTER 4

Hire Me— Strategic Ways to Land a Great Job

You cannot change the past, but anyone can start from now and create a whole new ending.
—ZIG ZIGLAR, AUTHOR AND SPEAKER

The biggest salary increases come from quitting your present job and going to work for a new employer. If you plan strategically, you can achieve this goal. But also consider that the new skills you've acquired and want to use, pursuing new interests, or the change you seek might actually exist in your current organization. Internal moves take some good self-marketing, but this can be a good solution, where all the company perks stay in place. There are times in our lives when a complete and total career change is the answer. Whichever route you choose to pursue, the most important first step in looking for a new job is to have a clear idea of the job target you want. You can't focus your efforts fully until you are clear on which job you are going after. Once you've decided on the targeted position (for example, marketing manager, purchasing agent), you're ready to move on, full speed ahead, to land the job.

You have special talents and abilities to offer an employer, but to market yourself successfully you must understand your true value. To get a better job, obtain a raise, or land a higher salary you must operate from the belief that you, as a worker, are talented and offer great value for your services. Employers pay more for perceived value, just as consumers pay more for products they perceive to be better. *Employers pay more for employees they place a higher value on.* Therefore, *do not* underestimate your value in the marketplace.

In the first few chapters, you took stock of your skills, also noting transferable skills—those traits and abilities you already possess that are marketable to a new employer. They can include management or computer skills, planning, research, budget analysis, organizing, scheduling, and so forth. These skills can often mean the difference between starting a new career over, at the bottom, or starting somewhere in the middle or at the top. For example, Nicholas went back to law school in his late forties. When he graduated, he found a law practice where he was pretty much left to himself to develop a client load. Having run a successful business before, he drew on all his previous skills. He had been politically active working on environmental issues as a passionate hobby. All of his contacts and political experience positioned him to be quickly hired as an environmental lobbyist. He fulfilled his dream of being able to really make a difference, working on creating, challenging, and defending environmental causes. Nicholas completely skipped over all the lean "rookie" years since he brought so many other skills and business contacts to the table. Transferable skills are the key to changing careers without having to start over at the bottom. Understanding the value of and *fully communicating to employers your transferable skills* is the key to maintaining, meeting, or even beating your salary goals. So the first step is to analyze your targeted job and review your background for transferable skills. Review your skills and strengths. Note any and all skills important in performing the job you desire now. Be sure to include management, computer, and technical skills you possess.

Identify and note your specialized industry skills and knowledge. You'll want to think about these skills so you can communicate them to employers in cover letters and resumés and certainly during any interviews.

Know Where to Look

Michael became my client when a merger at his parent company resulted in his termination. A controller, Michael had spent nine years with his employer before losing his position.

It left Michael feeling discouraged, depressed, disillusioned. He couldn't believe this all happened just months after he'd remarried. The resumés he'd sent produced no interviews, the executive recruiter hadn't been helpful at all, and Michael had that feeling of desperation that envelops many unemployed job hunters.

I explained to Michael that he needed to target a position, enter the hidden job market, and use persuasive self-marketing techniques. Michael quickly realized that he had *not* been looking for a job using the most effective tools. We created a new resumé and more effective cover letters. He was astounded to discover that the want ads, the Internet, or recruiters were not the only, or even the best, ways to find a job. *Fact: Labor studies reveal that 85% of all jobs are hidden and never advertised.*

Michael left my office with a clear action plan. He indeed found an exceptionally good job, one that was never advertised. He was excited about the new company and started the job making $18,000 more per year than he'd made in his old position.

There are many strategies that you can use to get an employer to call you in for an interview. In this chapter, I've outlined the most common ones, as well as the most effective. I recommend you adopt most, if not all, of the hidden job market techniques.

These uncover the truly outstanding jobs. Our first goal here is to uncover great jobs—interesting and appealing ones that get you excited just thinking about them. Don't hold yourself back. You *can* go after that dream job. These techniques will help you meet employers, talk to hiring managers, and do what Michael did—*find an exceptional job.*

Job-Hunting Strategies

Common Techniques

The Want Ads

Most hunters need a crash course on what works in today's competitive marketplace. Michael answered over one hundred ads, and for many of them he was either overqualified or very underqualified. He'd done no market research—it was more like a shotgun approach. He waited for the Sunday paper and spent many wasted hours applying for jobs he wasn't a good match for or felt depressed when there weren't many jobs listed.

Fewer than 15% of all jobs are ever advertised in the newspaper. And the number of want ads is shrinking in every newspaper in the country. More employers are recruiting online instead. Want ad jobs often elicit steep competition and many resumés. To save time and effort, follow this rule of thumb—respond to an ad only if you have the majority of the skills the employer is requesting. If they want eight years of experience and you have three, it's a very remote possibility that they'll select you from the competition, several of whom will have the requested eight years of experience.

This is an area where career changers often make big mistakes. They run after great-sounding jobs, but they have no direct experience. That combination rarely gets a phone call from an employer looking for the specific set of skills and experience advertised. True career changers (those seeking a whole new career field or activity) will find answering want ads very frustrating. For true career changers, time and energy is better spent on using the hidden job market techniques (unless you are planning to start at an entry-level position, in which case want ads can be helpful).

A lot of people apply for jobs they aren't qualified for. A client (a returning-to-work mom) once asked me to help with a cover letter for the job of director of student services for a local community college. I looked through the job description and asked her, "Do you have any program management experience? Have you supervised student programs before? Do you have a minimum of five years of experience working for a college?" She said no to each question, yet these were the three major requirements for a person to perform this job. She did add, "But I know I could do it." Maybe she could. But once the employer has gone to the newspapers, many will apply who have *already* done it. Sometimes you can stretch a bit, but if you're not even in the ballpark, don't waste your time writing cover letters and sending out resumés for jobs that you're not a solid match for. Having said this, I should add that many people, myself included, first learned about an opening from the newspaper, so try these tips for want ad success:

- Apply only for jobs for which you are adequately qualified.
- Write a targeted cover letter using the Power Impact Technique (which has a powerful opening sentence and is taught with numerous examples and employer insights in my book *Winning Cover Letters,* available on my website, www.robinryan.com).
- Use contacts and colleagues to provide "insider information" on the employer's true needs and concerns about performing the available job. Then specifically address those needs in your cover letter.
- Contact the employer directly, if possible, for a complete job description and more information about the position.

Human Resources

Microsoft's human resources department receives over twenty thousand resumés every month. That's a staggering amount, making it nearly impossible for applicants to get noticed. It's a mistake to just send resumés to dozens of companies' personnel offices, an error that many job hunters make. Human Resources role is to screen people *out*. Unless they have a job opening, your resumé is likely to be filed or tossed, never to be seen again.

Human resources staff can provide an excellent overview of the company, its organization structure, general job duties, and salaries/benefits. But you don't need to waste your time contacting a lot of human resources offices. There are more effective ways to job search, ways that actually put you in front of potential bosses, which I'll outline in a few pages. Always remember, *HR doesn't hire* (except for their own HR staff). Your success really depends on getting noticed by your true potential boss.

Temporary / Contract Work

Temporary or contract work allows you to gain valuable work experience. It gives you a chance to work inside a company and find out about positions you may be qualified for. Almost all companies use temporary workers from time to time. Many highly skilled professionals sell their services to earn income while they're looking for full-time employment. The trend for the next decade shows increasing use of professional temporary workers, in particular technical workers, but also engineers, programmers, nurses, systems analysts, accountants, project mangers, and numerous other specialty workers. These jobs pay very well but lack benefits and employer perks. Manufacturers, large companies, and high-tech organizations commonly fill their ranks with professional contract workers (another name for nonpermanent employees).

Temporary work is a great way to gain the inside track and potentially become a permanent employee. Once an employer has tried you out and believes that you are a good fit, the employer is happy to pay the finder's fee to your contract employment agency for the chance to hire you on permanently. Many clients, especially those changing careers and desiring to move into high-tech jobs, land great jobs starting as a contract temp worker. This is a proven way to get into great companies when entering a new field. It's also a great way into companies that have imposed temporary "hiring freezes."

Approach temporary work situations with a success strategy. Tell the temporary agency which companies you want to work for. Bring examples of your work, references, and a detailed resumé that describes the skills and abilities you can sell through the temporary agency. Your advantage once you work at a company is that you can learn about other openings. Your new supervisor might also be helpful in passing your resumé along to the right person.

Research temporary agencies, then develop a relationship with one to ensure you will be placed in the kinds of jobs you want. If your performance is good, it will guarantee a lot of future work with the agency. Experience, exposure, and job leads can result from doing temporary contract work, plus it pays the bills while you look for something else. Many people find temporary work to be a hiring "back door." So be sure to explore it as a potential option.

Executive Recruiters / Employment Agencies

Most recruiters or agencies specialize in a particular field. They *work for the employer* (that's who is paying their fee) to find an exact match for the employer's needs. Their service places middle, senior, and top executives. Recruiters are in the "hot fields"—high tech, finance, and CEO searches, for example—where employer demand creates a need and willingness to pay for their services. They service a small, elite group of job hunters, but their numbers are dwindling as more and more firms close shop. The reason is that companies have balked at paying exorbitant fees (usually 30% of the candidate's annual salary) in order to find talent. Most recruiters no longer work in firms but now work internally, as paid company employees within the human resources department.

Still, in some fields recruiters do exist as very small players. They seek and place people who have had *specific experience*. So for most career changers, recruiters will *not* be a useful resource. In the future, you will find that more and more "virtual" recruiters (online niche sites) are linking job seekers with employers.

TIPS FOR USING A RECRUITER SUCCESSFULLY

• Identify well-respected recruiters by asking colleagues and senior executives for referrals. A referral will pique the recruiter's interest more than just a cold call from you alone.
• Identify two or three companies you're interested in. Call their human resources department and ask for the names of the executive recruitment firm and individual they work with. This is a particularly helpful technique when you are seeking to relocate to a new city and may be completely unaware of who's who in that marketplace.

Beware Employment Rip-offs

A fool and his money are easily parted, and a desperate fool . . . well . . . you should avoid these rip-offs during your job search. Ignore ads that promise huge salaries and few work hours. (Most are multilevel marketing programs with big dollar investments required to "launch your business.") Bypass those consultants, firms, and outplacement organizations that charge exorbitant fees—$3,500–$10,000—to find you a job. These outfits prey on your vulnerability and defenselessness by claiming, "We've got all the contacts," or, "You don't need to do anything—we'll do it." The fine print in their contract never guarantees you a job. These firms often have many complaints and lawsuits against them from dissatisfied, and still unemployed, customers. *Money* magazine identified this type of employment scam as one of the top consumer rip-offs in America. Use only certified or reputable career counselors and thoroughly investigate exactly what you'll recieve for the amount invested.

Never pay for job information or employer lists, since most are available for free. Look online or ask a librarian to help you find the information you seek. Never pay a subscriber fee to electronic databases, resumé services, or online job banks until you've seen firsthand the quality and success of the product. Inquire as to how current the listings are, and ask for references in your field who have used the services effectively. Many associations offer resumé or job listing services that are reputable and nominally priced (and often available free to members).

Tapping into the Hidden Job Market

Want an inside view as to how and why the "hidden job market" is the best place to look for a great job?

Here's a firsthand glimpse into what a hiring manager is thinking and doing when faced with the need to add a new employee. Cynthia Richerman is director of engineering for a large manufacturer. She just learned that one of her best project managers is leaving. This is a big problem that she needs to solve ASAP.

"Terrific," Cynthia thinks sarcastically. "He couldn't pick a better time to quit. I'm plowed under with work, and now I'll need to pick up some extra workload. Kathleen and Daniel will need to put in overtime—we can't let the process systems project get behind." Exasperated, she lets out a long breath and resigns herself to the news. "Okay—got to hire someone. Let me get out that file with those people who've sent me resumés recently. . . . Hmmm," she ponders. "There's no one terrific here that could step in and fill Joe's shoes. I need to see if anyone else knows of someone who can help us."

A few hours later, Cynthia calls a meeting and addresses her staff: "Well, by now I'm sure you've heard Joe is moving on to a new city and job. I'm glad for him, but it will be a challenge for us to replace him. That's why I called you in here. Time is of the essence. You know if I have to go through HR it'll take forever to replace Joe. I want to speed that up and get someone on board in the next few weeks, if at all possible. We can't get behind now. Several of you will need to pitch in until someone new is on board. Here's what would help—please take some time and think of anyone who might be good for the job. You're all really familiar with the types of duties and skills we need a project manager to have. Call anyone who's good and have them fax a resumé and letter directly to me. Here's a memo you can send out that outlines the job. Try to think of some people—this is a top priority."

Cynthia heads back to her office and finds she has a message from Kent, an engineer she's on an association committee with. Calling him back, she tells him, "We're looking for a new project manager, Kent—do you happen to know of anyone we should consider?" Kent says, "No, not at this time." Cynthia calls a dozen colleagues over the next few days, with no luck. "I've got to get someone good," she says, feeling powerless to make the perfect project manager appear at her door.

At the start of the next week, Cynthia passes out her job opening memo at a department head meeting and sends it to the company's internal job listing service—a corporate website. After four weeks and considering three or four people who just weren't right, she sends her memo to the human resources department.

Three weeks later, the ad appears in the Sunday newspaper. It's another four weeks before human resources finally calls Cynthia to look at the resumes they've sorted out as good potentials from all they received. It takes another six weeks for interviews and selection before the new person starts. Cynthia is exhausted. She sits in her office reviewing the whole process. "I hate hiring," she thinks. "I've got so much to do and it takes so much time. In four months I've clocked nearly two hundred extra hours between work and the hiring stuff. I hope this new woman works out. I wish someone I knew had recommended her. I hope no one ever, ever quits again."

Cynthia is typical of most hiring managers. They find the entire process trying and somewhat exasperating. Once the boss knows they need a new employee, they want to hire someone fast to get on with the work. They also want someone "good" and wait to find the right candidate. When asking for referrals, they hope the person asked (who they assume is more familiar with the organization and job) will send a better potential employee their way. These two factors keep the hidden job market alive, well, and an active part of America's employment process.

The two major reasons the hidden market exists are time and better employee fits. So *concentrate your efforts on the hidden job market,* since most of the better jobs are found there. Networking is the best way to get in front of hiring managers and convince them of your transferable skills, as well as learn what they need, want, and value so you can relate your background to them in a way that's appealing.

By now you have read the information in the previous chapters intended to help you establish your job target and ideal job. You should have a clear focus. You need to know exactly what you are looking for so that these techniques can maximize your success.

The following chart shows exactly how the hiring process works, starting with the manager's need to hire someone. The normal process is for the manager to first think, "Who do I know who could do this job?" After that, the hiring manager will look over his or her records, ask staff, call colleagues (people the manager networks with and trusts), tell company employees, and place the job on the Web. If no good potential candidates turn up, the manager will then turn the whole thing over to the personnel department and try advertising in the newspapers. Entering the "hidden job market" means getting there before the crowd, because if the hiring manager finds a good candidate early on, the job never makes it to the newspaper classified ads. The "hidden job market" is operating before the position is formally advertised in the newspapers. This is the time to get in front of employers, since that's when most jobs are filled. The hidden job market is *the way* into many high-tech industries, Fortune 500 companies, emerging and fast-growth organizations, governmental positions, and nonprofit organizations.

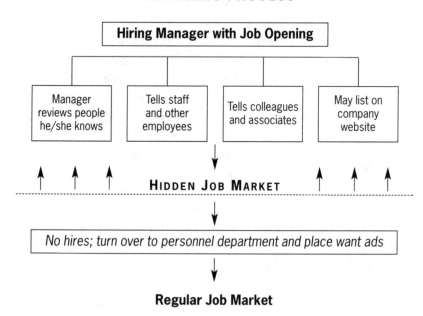

THE HIRING PROCESS

Hiring Manager with Job Opening			
Manager reviews people he/she knows	Tells staff and other employees	Tells colleagues and associates	May list on company website

HIDDEN JOB MARKET

No hires; turn over to personnel department and place want ads

Regular Job Market

Most Effective Techniques

The best way to achieve personal career satisfaction is to work for an organization you like and respect. *Job market research is es-*

sential. It allows you to identify a potential organization that meets your ideal company profile and look more closely at the company's culture to determine if you'd really like to work there.

Our purpose is to uncover potential job leads and the names of prospective employers. Job market research is done on the Internet, in the library, over telephones, and through conversations with colleagues, friends, and acquaintances.

Abundant sources of information exist, so to use your time effectively, seek some help from a reference librarian, who can quickly help you locate online resources and books, plus business directories, annual reports, magazine articles, employer databases, trade journals, and salary surveys—all are gold mines of potential job leads.

Make note of names, addresses, phone numbers, emails, and company websites. I recommend your local business journal as a valuable resource. In most cities, these journals rank local employers by fields, plus cover new products, services, and business changes. Whenever you read about a new store opening or a company expanding into a new service area, draw the conclusion that this means new jobs. Record information such as company size, growth potential, the name of the manager, anything that might help you make contact with the employer. For government listings and nonprofit organizations, try the Yellow Pages or their websites.

Any company that's publicly traded on the stock market has an annual report. Most companies now post theirs on their website, or you can call and request that it be sent to you. An annual report contains valuable information on company growth, new products and services, location of offices and plants, and future plans, as well as the names of top management officials. It's well worth reading.

Professional associations are a great source of information. Often they produce a directory, which lists companies or organizations, plus the names and phone numbers of people who work there. Association directories are an underused but valuable resource.

You can make contacts by attending meetings or annual conferences. Associations can provide excellent career information about the field, types of jobs, salary ranges, and future trends, and they usually have job listings. Association newsletters often have articles about people in the profession, and they help keep you up-to-date on current jargon. For example, a marketing director working in the grocery foods industry might wish to make a career change to the healthcare industry. He or she would need to conduct extensive market research and perhaps join one or more associations to gain knowledge about this new industry. Conducting informational interviews with association officers is always a good place to start. They are usually very knowledgeable about the field, and their duties as an officer include helping members (and potential members). They can become valuable contacts.

Ask family and friends for suggestions. Pay close attention to reputation, what others have heard about a company's workplace, to gain perspective.

While you're doing your research, you won't find a directory or article entitled "New Job Openings in the Hidden Job Market." You need to sharpen your detective skills in order to develop your list of potential employers to contact. Take time to read the past year's trade journals in your field and any pertinent magazine articles. Scan the economic news in newspapers. Go back several months, because there often are announcements of new developments and opportunities.

Build up a list of twenty or more potential employers. Too often a person has only one or two job possibilities, and when these prospects fall through it can be devastating. Knowing you have several other possibilities will soften the blow if a company passes you by and hires someone else.

Job market research will be an ongoing effort throughout your job search. Always ask friends, colleagues, and new contacts for recommendations—it's a great way to learn about new or smaller organizations you might otherwise miss. If you run out of leads, go back to the library or Internet and look again. The goal is to explore a multitude of companies to discover organizations that fit your ideal profile and whose corporate culture and products, services, and mission are of particular interest to you.

Networking

News flash: 63% of people hired in the last year found their job through contacts; 90% of our top executives said networking was important to their career rise; 68% listed it as very important. No one said it didn't matter. Every executive said it was at least mildly important to career success. You must learn to network. That's a key conclusion of our top executive survey.

Ed, an aerospace engineer, had no network to speak of and belonged to no professional or civic organizations. When a major layoff took his employer by storm, he had a difficult time. He told me, "I guess I really was remiss about developing a network. It didn't seem important. I wish I'd done it, because now I don't know how to start."

He tried a few colleagues, neighbors, and friends. I suggested he contact his college's alumni office to see if they had an alumni network in place that might help him. They did. A few alums offered to pass on his resumé, which led him to getting a terrific new job with Motorola.

Rachel, on the other hand, was a "networking queen." An executive director for a prestigious association, she generously helped everyone who knocked on her door. She also made professional friends as well as contacts. Twice she'd been approached by colleagues asking her to apply for a position, when she wasn't even looking for a new job. Both times she landed the job. Rachel's ongoing networking kept her visible—she was someone people thought of when they needed to hire a person in her capacity.

According to labor studies, 63% of all jobs in the last year were found through contacts. "People you know" plus "people you'll get to know" all lead to opening employers' doors, allowing you to discover great jobs and employers to discover talented people. Much has been written about networking and using contacts. This strategy begins with compiling a list of contacts. There's no magic or luck involved in putting together this list. Stop thinking, "I don't know anyone."

Start your contact list by listing everyone you *do* know—colleagues, former employees, school friends, former bosses, friends, neighbors, family, association executives, anyone you can think of. One client said she got an interview with the president of ABC News because her mother and the president's mother spend their winters together in the same Florida condominium complex and know each other. Never underestimate where a great connection might come from. A retired sixty-five-year-old grandma seemed an unlikely source for meeting top-notch business contacts—but for this client she was perfect! Remember, everyone knows someone, and it just may be that someone who can be of the most help to you.

Networking has changed a great deal over the years; it's no longer entrepreneurs trying to drum up business. It involves developing colleagues who can be a resource for you and to whom you can return the favor. A good network remains a career necessity. Our top executives and all career counselors recommend that you develop a strong network, one that will support and enhance your career in your current position and when seeking new opportunities.

To use your contacts effectively, don't approach any until you are ready. A common mistake, especially when people have just lost their jobs, is to frantically call *everyone* they've ever met and say, "I'm looking for a job—do you know of one?" Why is this a huge error? When you're not prepared, you often aren't articulating the specific job title, company, or kind of company you want. Don't waste the networking opportunity until you are prepared. That means having a resumé that's up-to-date and is the best marketing advertisement of your skills and abilities. It also means you ask for specifics from contacts, making it easier for them to help you. Define the job you are looking for, since they may not know exactly what a systems analyst or outreach counselor is or does. Educate them and then ask if they know of anyone who works at the list of companies you're interested in. Ask about the company's reputation, the "inside scoop," so to speak. And ask for referrals—people they know whom you should contact. This kind of networking will develop helpful contacts and valuable information on job leads and referrals that will open doors.

Informational Interviews

Informational interviews uncover unadvertised job openings. This technique—conducting fifteen- to twenty-minute interviews to obtain job, organizational, or industry information—is one of the more valuable techniques you can use. Barbara Hundley, associate chancellor at the University of Illinois, advises you to call and ask for a brief informational interview. You get fifteen to twenty minutes of undivided attention, allowing you to ask anything you want to know. Several CEOs noted that this direct approach worked, with the advantage being that this technique allows you to speak to hiring managers, business owners, and employers *directly.* You'll learn firsthand about their needs and which skills they value most. Labor studies reveal that 85% of all jobs are never advertised. The best way to find one is to research new companies or open positions through informational interviewing. This is how really great jobs are often found. Informational interviewing is a proven technique that job hunters have used for years. Although it's been popular since the mid-1980s, I still find that many people in my job search classes have never heard of it. The technique consists of this: *Arrange and conduct a short fifteen- to twenty-minute interview to learn more about potential job openings, valued skills, and a company's structure or culture.*

There are several levels of effective informational interviewing, and for a career changer there is no more valuable tool available for use.

- **Basic Informational Interviewing** provides insight for the career changer who is researching a new career field or industry. In this kind of interviewing, you want to talk to people who are actually doing the job you'd like to do, in the field you'd like to be in. You can assess what the job duties are and which skills are needed for the position. You explore salary, educational requirements, and the normal career track that leads to this kind of position. You can have them identify the transferable skills you possess that would serve you in the new field. You can learn how someone might enter the field or advance his or her career in the industry. Basic Informational Interviewing allows you to gather knowledge to determine whether you want to change fields, enter a new field, or work in a specific industry by learning "the real scoop" on the potential job. You'll uncover specific job requirements, organizational structure, locations, departments, products, and decision makers' names, and you'll discover where job openings might be. Ask any contact at a company, and he or she can give you insight into the company culture—how it does its hiring, where your job might fall in the organizational structure, who might hire for that kind of position. Additionally, you want to ask for the names of the hiring decision makers.

- **Job-Hunting Informational Interviewing** is the next level, where you actually set up appointments with the people who have the power to hire you at the organizations where you wish to work. This is where you learn from your potential boss about his needs and the skills he values. This is the stage that many of you may jump to immediately. Your conversations will uncover job leads and important selling points to market the skills and talents employers care about.

Here's how to do it. Make the initial appointments through an introductory letter or phone call, *using the contact's name as a referral*. State the purpose for the meeting—here, the truth works well. Tell the person you'd like advice on a job search or are thinking about changing careers to one similar to hers and would love some firsthand insights. Another lead-in might be your desire to obtain information on a field or new industry, or the news that you're planning to relocate to the person's area. Be sure to make it clear that you seek a brief meeting (fifteen, no more than twenty minutes) and don't expect to hear about a job opening, but are simply looking for guidance and input to help you better direct your job search or career change.

Most informational interviews are done on the phone, but on rare occasions you may meet at the person's office or for lunch. With online instant messaging gaining popularity, this option might also work for you. Although straight email doesn't allow for the give-and-take that extensive questions require, for a quick question or two, email may be a viable way to conduct a brief interview and get a lead.

Prepare for the interview by reading company literature and visiting its website. Know what information you plan to request. Write out your questions, which may include queries into job duties, major responsibilities, salary ranges, function or structure of organization, corporate culture, trends in the field, and procedures, products, and programs in use or development. You might also ask about sources of additional information, contacts or companies to consider, and any suggestions they may have for entry into or development of a particular position, field, industry, or company.

Start your informational interview by taking 60 seconds to reintroduce yourself and explain your reason for being there, summarizing your background and credentials. This will save time and allow you to ask specific questions and get answers in the time allotted. Be sure to ask for referrals and talk about other companies to approach. Be prepared and conscious of the time.

If you go past the agreed-upon minutes, offer to arrange a second meeting so as not to put the person out or cause him or her to work overtime because of you.

Some of these contacts are better than others. I remember one time I obtained an informational interview, and the man was forty minutes late for our appointment, rote, uninterested, and not helpful at all. I did ask him for the names of a few other people I should contact. He referred me to Penny, a high-level TV executive, who became one of the best resources I've ever met. She gave me terrific insider information, solidified some of my transferable skills, and pointed out how to sell myself and break into the industry. I later learned she had a reputation for being enormously helpful—so you never know where one contact will lead you. As for Penny, beyond a thank-you note I never was able to pay her back, but the universe did. She's continued to move up and up, and last I heard, she held a fabulous position at the Fox network. Helping others pays off, because other people will help you.

In a perfect world, every contact would open his door and let you drop by. He'd offer wonderful insights and several job leads and provide you with contact names. Many of my clients find this is exactly what happens. But often, busy executives are reluctant to invite you to their offices. Maybe people overstayed their welcome in the past, resulting in one or even two hours spent helping someone. Today, many are cautious and need to monitor their time more wisely, due to their own job demands. Although face-to-face meetings allow an up-close look at both the person and the company, simple telephone chats work well, too. You can learn a lot either way, and fifteen minutes on the phone is ideal if you are already employed, with little time of your own to spare.

Informational interviewing as a type of networking is a very effective way to learn about openings and the exact skills employers value and hire for. Use it often and wisely. Always be sure to send a thank-you note with a business card inside. No business card? Then create one on your computer or have inexpensive ones printed, with your name, address, home phone, and email on them.

In order to get useful answers, ask good questions! You're in the driver's seat, but since time is short, ask your most important questions first.

TYPICAL QUESTIONS YOU MIGHT ASK:

- What are the most important skills necessary for success in this job?
- What is the most pressing problem or challenge the field faces?
- I anticipate the salary range for this job to be between $40,000 and $45,000. Is that about right, or is it too low or high?
- Tell me more about . . .
- What are your current growth plans?

Don't waste people's time. They've been generous enough to assist you. Be prepared to make the most of the meeting by mapping and prioritizing your questions in advance.

There are two important steps to complete during an informational interview. First, discuss your employer prospect list. Ask your contact if he knows anyone who works for any of the companies listed and if he can think of any other companies you should add to your prospect list. Second, inquire about any other people he can think of whom you should meet who could help you.

If you are fortunate enough to meet at the person's place of employment, you'll benefit from an inside view of the company's corporate culture. Upon completion of any informational interview, write about what you've learned, which skills your contact thought were important. Note your impressions of the position or company. Do it immediately, so you don't forget anything. Many companies are jettisoned from a potential employer list after job hunters get a brief look inside and don't like what they see.

Always send a thank-you note to anyone who helps you. A handwritten note is the most impressive—emails are too informal and a very poor substitute for the real thing.

Targeted Mailings

Self-marketing letters, sent to specifically targeted employers and followed up properly, can open some impressive doors to future jobs. One retail buyer who was downsized used this technique to get interviews with the head buyer for Macy's, Bloomingdale's, and Lord & Taylor after all her efforts through the personnel departments yielded big fat zeroes.

This approach focuses on obtaining accurate information such as names, titles, and addresses of people with the power to hire you. A quick phone call can identify the correct person to address the letter to and weed out those organizations that don't have an appropriate job or division. For instance, some positions may exist only at company headquarters and not at regional offices near where you live.

The next step is to mail queries to potential bosses within a well-researched, small group of employers. You must mail to the correct person, specifically the potential boss or the hiring manager, *not* the human resources department. Your cover letter should be targeted and laced with your top abilities—an introduction that includes a resumé. End the letter stating you'll call in a few days—and then do so. Begin your conversation by stating who you are and inquiring whether the person has received your letter. Then ease into a sixty-second pitch on your background and ask what his current needs may be. If he starts to chat, you could have a prospect. If he says, "We aren't hiring," take a moment and see if you can't produce a job lead. Ask him if he might know of anyone who is looking for someone with your skills. This closing question has often produced solid leads for my clients, many of whom found a job from the recommended source. This follow-up call must be direct. Avoid leaving a message—you don't want a potential employer calling back and catching you off-guard and unprepared. Just before eight A.M., immediately after five P.M., or during the lunch hour are all times you often catch people at their desk answering their own phone. Don't be timid about this approach. Keep in mind there is always a demand for dedicated, enthusiastic workers.

Not sure it will work? Michelle sent a dozen letters over a four-week period and followed up with calls to each hiring manager. She had a particularly difficult time reaching one manager, calling on numerous occasions (but not leaving her name). Finally, they connected. Someone had just quit, and she got invited in for an interview. Three days later, Michelle started as the firm's new executive account representative, with a company car and high base salary, in a completely different industry. Michelle's experience validates that the extra time spent to make your career move does pay off.

Targeted Mailings Success Secrets

- Create a targeted letter that specifically identifies the job you seek and summarizes your strongest skills to perform the job.
- Mail the letter with a resumé to the department head or hiring manager directly.
- State in the letter that you'll call in a few days to learn more about the manager's current needs.
- Make the follow-up call. Don't leave a message. Continue to call until you reach the manager.
- Get a referral if no opportunities exist at this organization.
- In large companies, ask for referrals to other appropriate department heads or managers and then immediately contact them.

For examples of effective targeted letters, check out my book *Winning Cover Letters* at my website, www.robinryan.com.

Internet

Is the Internet the *best* way to find a job? Clients and seminar participants continue to affirm my long-held belief that visiting big websites like Monster.com often proves to be an enormous time waster. It's just not productive. A faster way to find out about openings is to go directly to a company's website and look at its listings. Also, niche or vertical sites—those advertising for a specific field like engineering or sales—are fast becoming excellent job locators. Professional associations offer niche sites, so try your state's professional associations—for instance, the bar association, CPA society, and so on—which will have better lists with more applicable potential openings. Employers target these groups because they reach the exact people they are trying to hire. Niche sites should be looked at often—they can and will have good potential jobs to apply for. As more Americans head online, many view the Internet as *the* job source of the future. Indeed, hundreds of thousands of jobs are listed on the Internet, but that doesn't mean the ones *you seek* are there. The majority of jobs listed on the Internet are advertising for jobs you don't want—or they're based in Topeka, Detroit, Lancaster, or somewhere else you don't want to live. Small companies are very unlikely to conduct "electronic searches" unless they are in the high-tech arena. The fact remains that a high-percentage of all new jobs created last year were with small employers (fewer than one hundred employees). Large companies may accept resumés through the information superhighway, but sending a resumé that is electronically received and then "scanned" by the personnel department has proven to be a very *ineffective* job hunting method. Writing directly to the hiring manager (your potential boss) using a targeted snail mail letter (or even email) has repeatedly produced much better results.

The Internet is a terrific source of information about jobs, companies, cities, and fields. The Internet has *proven* itself to be a great research tool, saving job seekers tremendous amounts of time, money, and aggravation during their initial job market or career field search. Many clients report that they've found extensive employer information and critical salary surveys on the Internet.

You'll find that visiting a company's website is an efficient way to find job openings (try using the company name as the URL address—for example, www.americanexpress.com). Many companies, governmental agencies, and nonprofits now post all their job listings on their own website. Specific niche, often called vertical, sites are a better choice when using the Internet to job hunt. It's well worth the effort to place your resumé on sites dedicated to your particular field. Professional associations often list job openings on their sites. Most clients report that spending dozens of hours on massive sites like Monster.com, which lists a million jobs, usually results in wasted time and almost never yields interviews.

A word of caution: Searching the Internet for job openings can eat up a great deal of time. *This remains the biggest drawback concerning the Internet.* You must talk to employers in order to get hired. So use the bulk of your time actively looking and talking, or you'll end up frustrated. Too much time spent posting resumés online, with little response, can make you feel as if yours were swallowed into a black hole, never to be seen again. Resumé blasting, which is bombarding sites everywhere, will not get you hired and is a waste of your time and money. Never send resumés as email attachments. Paste them inside your emails to insure they will be read. With all the viruses out there, many companies simply block attachments; it's also possible for an attachment to get scrambled in transmission because you created it in a different software, such as Works, and not the universal corporate word-processing software, Word.

The Internet has changed its face in the five seconds that it took me to write this sentence. Despite its drawbacks, the Internet is a significant source of job leads and is growing in usage every day. Niche sites and companies' websites are the ones to concentrate on.

Is a Company's Culture the Right Fit for You?

Recently a new client called, desperate to speak to me. Tom explained that he'd just started a new job ten days ago, and had he realized what it was going to be like, he'd never have accepted the position. The job was awful. He was in a panic and needed help.

Tom made a costly mistake by not thoroughly determining the company's culture and atmosphere before he accepted the job. Every organization has a workplace environment that defines what it is actually like to work there. Often you have preconceived ideas about a company that prove to be inaccurate once you get into the interview and begin to ask your questions. The trick is to ask the right questions and pay close attention to the answers to learn whether a prospective job is a good fit.

You can't always have prepared these questions in advance. They often emerge during the interview or networking process when something is mentioned in conversation. It's generally best to ask these questions as soon as they come up, saying, "Could you explain that more fully?" or, "Please elaborate." Be sure you get answers to inconsistencies or if a red flag comes up. Use your detective skills to determine what the true workplace environment will be and if it's a comfortable fit for you.

The best questions to ask are those designed to gather details on doing the job and about the organization's work culture and environment, to help you determine if this is a good job for you. Be sure to ask the appropriate question to the correct person Technical questions and job specifics are unlikely to be answered by the HR person, whose responsibility is to screen and validate your true experience, but who possesses only a general idea of the job's duties. You'll get the best answers asking potential bosses and employees who work inside the company, especially if they know the department where you'd like to be. By the end of your questions with the hiring manager or decision maker, you should know whether you want to work there or not. Here are a few questions you might want to bring up:

- What are the day-to-day responsibilities that I'll have in this job?
- Could you describe to me your typical management style and the type of employee who works well with you?
- What are some of the skills and abilities you see as necessary for someone to succeed in this job?
- What challenges might I encounter if I take on this position?
- What is your company's policy on providing seminars, workshops, conferences, and training so the employees can keep up on their skills or acquire new skills?
- Are there any restraints or cutbacks planned that would decrease budgets?
- How would you describe the corporate culture here?

You may wait to ask a few questions about the politics and current challenges until after you've been offered the job. Before you accept, it's wise and useful to get answers to questions such as "Tell me about the office politics here" or "As my new boss, could you explain your goals and management style and describe the attributes of people you work best with?"

Ask lots of questions about flextime, family-friendly policies, and overtime expectations. Many companies offer compensation time but discourage you from taking it. That means you can work the extra ten to twenty hours per month, but no one ever expects you to take that time off. That's a problem for a working parent who may need to take a child to the doctor or dentist or who wants to attend school events.

A family-friendly policy is no guarantee that, in practice, a business really is family friendly. One family broke up when the husband's new employer required Saturday night stays to get cheap airfare. This kept him away from his family for weeks at a time. It was also lonely for him being in the corporate center on the East Coast. So, while his wife and kids lived in Texas, he killed the time during those mandatory stays with new work friends. He went out socializing a lot and eventually found himself having an affair he'd never even thought he was capable of. Word to the wise—be sure you have a clear picture of the company's travel policies if you'll be traveling as a part of the job. Make sure they have your best welfare at heart.

Build an accurate picture of a company's work culture. This allows you to find a job and workplace that you'll really like and be satisfied going to daily.

Relocation—How to Find a Job When You Tag Along

We've hit an all-time high of employees turning down jobs that require relocation. The major reason: Their families didn't want to go. One client's horror story began with a heavy push by senior management on her engineer husband to accept a promotion, leave Birmingham, and move to midstate Pennsylvania. This would be the third move in five years, and Linda was reluctant to go. Her husband accepted the promotion with the stipulation that he could return within the year if his family didn't like the area. Linda, head of the aerobics program at a very exclusive gym, very reluctantly quit and moved her three kids to Pennsylvania.

Four months later, everyone was unhappy. The town was small and rural, and Linda couldn't find a job. Her husband traveled and was gone a great deal of the time. The kids hated the weather and longed for the warmth of the South. Linda issued

an ultimatum: We are moving back. When her husband talked to
his boss, he was flatly told no. He felt betrayed, since three other
employees had refused to move to Pennsylvania before him, and
now the company was going back on its word. He was stuck in
an impossible situation.

So what happened? Linda moved back to Birmingham with
the kids and even got her old job back. Her husband argued for
and got a severance package and followed her within the month.
It was a pretty expensive and stressful lesson on how a relocation
almost destroyed a five-person family.

It's usually women who find themselves as the "tagalong
spouse," but men are beginning to play this role, too. Dual careers
often have opposing paths, so here are some guidelines to help
you decide if the spouse's new job is worth it and how to get a job
for yourself once you get there, if you're the one tagging along.

- **Research the area thoroughly before you move.** Subscribe
  to local newspapers and order telephone directories. Write to
  the Chamber of Commerce for employment information.
  Visit your local library to investigate the types of employers in
  the region, predominant industries, companies, nonprofits,
  and so forth. Visit the area once or twice, and stay more than
  a day to be better able to weigh pros and cons. If you have
  kids, go to the local schools to get a sense of whether your
  children will be able to adjust easily.

- **Use the Internet.** Go to a search engine and type in the state
  and city you plan to move to. You'd be amazed at how much
  information is now available, so begin compiling a list of potential employers that would have the type of job you seek.
  Post your resumé online on bulletin boards and especially on
  employers' websites.

- **Ask for spouse career counseling.** Get in writing that an expert can help you develop a top-notch resumé and cover let-

ter. Work with someone in the new city before you get there
to help you develop a list of prospective companies, and start
job hunting before you go. At the very least, take a local job
search class once you get there. I have counseled many "taga-
longs" in sessions that were covered by the spouse's employer
as part of the relocation package.

- **Use pros to move you.** Companies often drop large bonuses
  on you, from which you cover all moving expenses. It is
  tempting to keep a big part of the cash and pack and unpack
  everything yourself. This is an enormous, draining task and
  often keeps you, the nonworking spouse, out of the job market for several months. It'll also add to your depression and
  sense of being overwhelmed. Stand strong and resist your
  spouse's argument, realizing that it is *you* who will have to do
  all of this draining work. Moving is stressful enough—try not
  to make it worse.

- **Build a new network.** As noted, fully 85% of all jobs are hidden or unadvertised, so networking is essential to your success.
  Ask everyone you know for names of anyone living in your
  new location. A key is to target a specific job. Contact your
  professional associations for state and city chapters to learn
  how they may be able to help you in your job search. Also
  check with your college for alumni who live in your new
  area—most have volunteers ready to help you job hunt. Once
  you arrive in your new city, join a professional group, church,
  or activity so you can make new acquaintances quickly.

Summary

Don't wait for employers to find you. Try these techniques, set
goals, do the extra work. Uncovering the "hidden job market" is

extra work—hard work with no immediate payoff. But consider the odds—85% of all jobs are here, and the crowd is *not*. It's only you and a few others and some terrific jobs just waiting for you to land them.

I've received hundreds of testimonials from clients that these techniques worked well and aided them in landing terrific jobs. They found better openings with better companies. *Be proactive and take control of your future.* Put in the extra effort required to find the most rewarding job possible, one that addresses your salary goals and family needs, and gets you the quality of life you want. Write out your goals and create a daily, weekly, and monthly action plan. You'll accomplish more once you've determined exactly where you are going and what you need to do to get there.

Success is always inside each of us. You just have to reach down inside and find it.
—JOE MONTANA, SUPERSTAR NFL QUARTERBACK

CHAPTER 5

Launching a Business

Accept the challenges so that you may
feel the thrill of victory.
—GENERAL GEORGE S. PATTON

"All I've ever wanted to do was feed people," said Gene Basco, a successful restaurant owner. "This is a hard business to make it in—you gotta love it, 'cause it's risky and a helluva lot of work, but I never wanted to do anything else."

"My father was a doctor with his own practice. I saw how much Dad helped people get and stay healthy, and knew that was my calling, too," said Dr. Kim Shara.

"I just love baseball—always have," said Allen Allsbrook. "I knew all the players and stats when I was a child. I wasn't that good at the sport, but I was glued to the TV set, following the Yankees' every move. Opening my own sports card store grew out of my love for the game. I'd never have made it if I didn't alter my plan and become one of the major Topps [baseball cards] distributors worldwide. All in all, I'd do this job for free, just so I could talk about baseball with folks—it's my whole universe, and every day I thank my lucky stars I'm in the middle of it."

You gotta love it!

There is no other way to start up, build, and succeed in your own business. Doctors, counselors, accountants, consultants, entrepreneurs, lawyers, graphic designers, dentists, florists, photographers, and interior designers—if they venture out on their own, the impetus is to do something they really love. These people often go on to build very successful small businesses, some making millions per year. Successful business owners all say, "It starts with a burning desire."

Success stories abound, big and small. Maybe you'll begin the next Microsoft or Ben & Jerry's. If you're willing to work for your dream, it can come true.

Debbie Coleman is a unique CEO—she starts companies, grows them into major, multimillion-dollar entities in four or five years, then leaves, finds a new one, and does it again. She's forty-six, and she's done this six times thus far. "If your goal is to make it to the big time, your real career goal is to be a CEO, with the job of running a business" stated Coleman. She shared some key lessons on how to take a start-up from nothing to a multimillion-dollar company. She advised, "You need experience at running a business and knowing how businesses operate. It's best to first get some experience working for someone else, learning on their dime. You need to admit you don't know everything and seek out advisers and mentors in other areas who do. I hire a team of people who have been successful in their areas, be it sales, operations, or distribution, because I know I cannot do it all myself, and I don't plan to. I develop a business plan and clear vision right from the start to keep everyone on focus. You must be disciplined enough to stay focused on goals, yet open enough and not so rigid that you'd stifle creativity or new ideas from others. A key secret of success is being open to new ideas while staying focused on what's best for the company. As a CEO building a new company, you must be the leader and teacher of the big picture, keeping your growing team in line with it," she said.

"You cannot grow your enterprise into a big company if as

CEO you think it's all got to be just you," Coleman continued. "With that attitude your business will remain small. Only by duplicating yourself and hiring smart people you can delegate to, people who will push the company to the next level, will you successfully build it bigger and bigger. Employees must buy into your vision and be entrusted to perform to their best. Reorganize and plan for the fact that you won't be able to maintain a total hands-on operation once it surpasses a certain success and revenue level."

Well, maybe you have less lofty goals. But Coleman's advice rings true no matter what. If you start a business—any business—your job is CEO of running it. Do you have a burning desire? Do you want to run your own show? Maybe head a consulting firm or build a mega-organization? Are you prepared to invest all the hard work, effort, and money necessary to succeed? Are you willing to sacrifice to make it happen? Will you spend the endless hours to learn what you don't know? Will your family support and help you once they realize your business takes a great deal of time away from them?

These are all good questions, because running a business is challenging and, at times, lonely and isolating. There are many things you'll do that you won't get paid for, like bookkeeping and banking—time-consuming tasks that must get done. On the upside, owning your own business can be the most rewarding thing you've ever done, and it can make you rich, too.

This chapter will provide you with an overview. Its purpose is to guide you in the decision-making process. It's not a start-up guide; it doesn't teach you how to write a business plan, nor does it cover how to fund the venture beyond some basic guidelines. There are dozens of books devoted to the subject of actually starting the business, and I've suggested several under "Recommended Resources." My goal is to give you clear insight into considering a business of your own, to help you explore your options, and to learn what it takes, what you must sacrifice, and what you will gain.

Whether your goal is to be a consultant, run a dress shop, open a law practice, or sell millions of whatever product you sell—somewhere, somehow, you must take the risk and challenge, go off on your own, and make it happen. Proceed wisely. To add to your probability of success, learn as much as you can about your new business—the craft, profession, trade, industry— and then get experience. This will help buffer the transition period, during which your business management skills are every bit as important to success as your product or service.

Last year, 898,000 Americans started their own businesses, according to the Small Business Administration. Unfortunately, 80% will fail or close within the first five years. This failure rate can be attributed to two major reasons: first, the business was underfinanced; and second, the owner underestimated the long hours required to operate the business and overestimated the take-home profit, which is usually much lower than hoped for.

All businesses have overhead—telephones, office equipment, taxes, advertising expenses—which must be paid before the owner gets paid. A solid business plan that includes conservative growth and realistic budgets is a much-needed road map to your success. You must determine the best location for your business. Currently, twenty-seven million people operate a business from home. The advantages include lower overhead, no lost commuting time, convenience, more personal profits, ability to work around family needs and schedules, and lower or more modest start-up costs.

Many new businesses opt to work from home. The single biggest complication, though, is how your business will impact your family and personal life. Motivated, driven people never worry about allowing house stuff to distract them from business responsibilities. On the contrary, they often find that the "ease" of going to the "office" equates to working *all the time*. Your business will never be out of sight. Whenever you pass by your "office," even if the door is closed, you'll know work is waiting. You must set parameters that you and your family can live with.

A separate phone line, designated hours, and respect for your "work time" are essential.

Another disadvantage is that working from home can be lonely and isolating. Some people aren't bothered by this, while others cite it as a big reason to go back into the corporate world, working for someone else. To combat this isolation, developing a network is a must.

If you choose to locate your business outside of your home, then you need to predetermine the resulting operating and start-up costs, which will include rent and utilities, to name two. It is essential to identify all these costs and plan accordingly in order to keep your business running during the first few lean years.

Not sure if this is the road for you? Take the business ownership assessment test to see if opening and running a business might be the perfect job for you.

Business Ownership Assessment

1. *Are you a self-starter?* It will be up to you, not someone else, to develop the business, organize the projects, manage your time, and follow through on details.
2. *Can you handle the uncertain financial risk?* Businesses all have cycles—ebbs and flows in profitability. Once it's started, you'll have overhead and operational expenses that must be met before you get paid.
3. *Do you have good business skills—accounting, business planning, operations, sales, marketing, and customer service?* You must attract customers. New and repeat customers are your business's lifeblood. You must possess or learn these skills to survive and succeed.
4. *Do you have the stamina needed to run a business?* Business ownership is a lot of work. Can you face twelve-hour workdays, six or seven days a week, every week?

5. *Are you motivated by achievement?* Many entrepreneurs get
   great joy out of the daily "wins" they get from running their
   business. They find it's a competitive game and a satisfying
   way to fulfill their instinct to achieve. They have fun doing it.
   These people have a passion and driving desire to come in
   first. They are doers and want to derive benefits from their
   efforts and labor. They are unlikely to get "burned out" or
   worn down by carrying all the responsibilities of the business
   on their shoulders. To build a big business, the passion must
   burn within you.

6. *Are you a good decision maker?* Business owners are required
   to make decisions constantly, quickly, under pressure, and in-
   dependently. Do you research and examine all options on important decisions to minimize your risk but then decide and
   go forward?

7. *How well do you handle different personalities?* Business owners
   need to develop working relationships with a variety of people, including customers, vendors, staff, bankers, and professionals such as lawyers, accountants, or graphic artists. Your
   ability to deal successfully with demanding clients, unreliable
   vendors, or cranky staff people in order to benefit your business will directly impact your success.

8. *How will the business affect your family?* It's hard to balance
   work and family demands during the first few years after
   starting a new business. There may also be financial difficul-
   ties until the business becomes profitable, which could take
   months or years. You may have to adjust to a lower standard
   of living or put family assets at risk. Can your family deal
   with the challenges business ownership requires? Although
   many entrepreneurs go on to make large incomes, the "lean
   years" are a necessary part of the evolution and business
   growth cycle. Equally important to consider are the many job
   perks—paid vacations, sick days, medical and dental insurance, stock options, cars, health club memberships—that dis-

appear when you own the company. Think about the extra costs you will now incur.

9. *How will you deal with the isolation and/or change in status?* Once you go off on your own, you'll be just that—*ALONE*. Can you deal with being isolated? Will you miss the status, respect, and collegial connections that you had while working for an employer other than yourself? Don't underestimate this—it's the reason many consultants and service business owners close their own operations and reenter the corporate world.

Key Mistakes to Avoid in Running a Business

"It's the passion burning within you, the fire in your belly, that causes you to put in all the effort to create great new things," said CEO Debbie Coleman. Nothing could be more true than that. Mark LeBlanc, author of *Growing Your Business* (www.smallbusinesssuccess.com), spent nineteen years assisting people who wanted to operate their own business.

"A key mistake in the beginning phase is to overlook the true start-up and operating costs," he said. "You say, 'I want to make $10,000 per month'—if that's the case, you'll need to generate between $20,000 and $30,000 a month to net $10,000. Your plan to build the business must include long-term cash for overhead. This is something most people don't acknowledge or see at the beginning. Many professional doctors, lawyers, accountants, and consultants miss this fact. The new business will take months, even years, before you get past spending start-up funds on operating overhead. This is a lesson many experience firsthand—you can't fall short, because the money you'll need to pay the bills won't be there."

According to the Small Business Administration, 30% of all

small businesses fail within the first year. LeBlanc said business owners must recognize that their new career is just that—*a career as a business owner.* You must learn about operations, accounting, marketing, sales, and service. Mastering these skills is more important than simply focusing all your attention on being an expert or good at your craft.

LeBlanc pointed out other mistakes people make when launching a business. Thinking they can go it alone, new business owners don't reach out for help, neglecting to ask for marketing advice or input from graphic artists, business coaches, or accountants. "Surrounding yourself with the right team and resources to run it" is essential, said LeBlanc.

Not learning how to communicate with customers or prospective customers is another common mistake. "Marketing just gets people in the door, but selling gets them to buy," he said. Selling can and must be learned. You have to give customers a reason to open their pocketbooks. Many new owners are actually timid, even afraid, to talk to customer prospects. Business owners want to place ads in the paper and have customers call and say, "Here's the money," not, "Tell me about your product or service." But that's how it works. Marketing leads customers to inquire, then you and/or your representatives must be able to SELL. "If not, you'll be busy answering phones, but earning no money."

Inconsistency can undermine all of your efforts. No matter how good you are, you never arrive at, and then rest on, success. "What are you doing every thirty days to market yourself?" LeBlanc asked. "Occasionally you get a big blip—but not on average. Ten calls a month will give you a stronger foundation than one hundred calls in one month, followed by none the rest of the year. Consistency is key—every thirty days do some marketing strategy. As soon as you stop marketing, within ninety days your business starts to dry up. Marketing is always and forever," he advised. It's the first and foremost ingredient for ongoing success in business.

"In nineteen years as a small-business consultant, I've seen many people taken in by the get-rich-fast MLM [multilevel marketing] or the networking business. The promise always exceeds what people really earn. The chances of *big* success are like playing the lottery," stated LeBlanc.

Young businesses evolve and grow, especially when you react to a market opportunity. Most people fantasize that they'll just open the business and get rich quick. That's a serious mistake! Most really successful businesses took a long while to get there. Paulette Ensign, a very successful small-business owner, shared the *real* journey she's gone through to reach the top, and there are several key lessons to learn from her story.

"My organizing business was already eight years old when I got the idea to produce a booklet on organizing tips. It took six months from starting to write the booklet until the first three dollars arrived.

"Months later, I had sold about 15,000 copies, at $3 each, one copy at a time. But when I checked my financial records, I realized I had tediously generated not a lot of money. After assessing the situation, I realized that during this time, I had recorded an audio program based on the booklet, gotten a contract from a company to write a booklet more specific to their product line, and begun teaching paid seminars to people who had bought the booklet.

"One day, a guy I know from a major consumer mail-order catalog company said: 'Why don't you license us reprint rights to your booklet? We can buy print cheaper than you, so if you charge us a few cents a unit, you wouldn't have to do production.' We exchanged a ten-page contract and a five-digit check. They provided the booklet free with any purchase in one issue of their catalog and saw a 13% increase in sales that issue. They were happy. I was happy.

"Next, I designed a class on how to write and market booklets and wrote an eighty-page manual. I now had another new product, an eighty-page manual, a blueprint for how I had sold more than 50,000 copies of my booklet without spending a penny on advertising. From there I went online to market my business. An Italian businessman made a deal to translate, produce, and market my booklet, paying me royalties on all sales. He wired several thousand dollars to my checking account after he made a sale of 105,000 copies to a magazine.

"Overall, I had sold more than 400,000 copies of my booklet, in two languages, without spending a penny on advertising. I never could have written a business plan for how all this has unfolded," concluded Paulette, who was an elementary school music teacher before she made a career change and opened her organizing business. "But it took a lot of hard work, effort, and time before I really profited from it."

Paulette's story is told in detail to illustrate several business lessons and facts about owning, operating, and succeeding at your own business:

- Businesses evolve and grow over time, but only if you can adapt, recognize market opportunities, and capitalize on them. You must continue to innovate, improvise, and be creative as long as you own the business.
- Most businesses are built on hits—singles and doubles—with an occasional home run here and there. Business owners looking only for grand slams may win a game but will usually miss the singles that eventually add up and take the business to a winning series.
- You need to be in it for the long haul and be willing to create products that require much time and effort to develop before anyone pays you a dime.
- You must think globally—the Internet has created a level playing field, allowing even the smallest companies to attract customers from all over the world.
- Constant marketing and creative promotional efforts are needed on a continuous basis to grow, expand, and maintain the venture.

The bottom line is this: You need to be in a business you are interested in and enjoy so you'll continue to expend the effort needed to make it succeed and go beyond that. Paulette was in business for eight years before she hit upon the "booklets" idea. She also tried something new—developing the booklets and creating a seminar/tape series, all at her own expense. Companies require capital investments, not just at the start but on a regular basis. New equipment, developing a website, and creating more products or services all come long before any dollars are made from them.

Paulette's true career is running a business. She's a great marketer and learned to capitalize successfully on opportunities that she made by networking, self-promotion, use of the Internet, and word-of-mouth advertising. You'll need to do that, too. Realize that her success wasn't an overnight phenomenon, it came after years of effort, and it's still ongoing today.

In conclusion, your own venture is something that, once started, will always require your time, money, and effort to reach and maintain both the income and the success you desire.

Start-up Options

Peter Drucker, management consultant and author, said, "Whenever you see a successful business, someone once made a courageous decision." Starting a business from scratch is the hardest and riskiest of ventures. While many people do this and succeed, there are other options that can make it easier. Consider these as you make your decisions.

Franchises

Of all the options for starting up your own business, franchises have the highest percentage of success. In fact, according to the

International Franchise Association, franchised retailers earned over $1,000,000,000,000—yes, $1 trillion—last year. Their estimated growth rate is 8.5% over the next several years. There are more than 2,500 different kinds of business franchise companies to consider and buy. More than 600,000 franchises—employing more than nine million people—are already open for business.

Franchising is a method of doing business. You buy into a national or international organization and then open up a storefront (by opening a retail operation, setting up a distributorship, or obtaining licenses to use the company's trademark brand name in conjunction with your business).

There are so many franchises available, you can easily find one that matches your interests. Some popular franchises include H&R Block, Wendy's, Homes and Land Publishing, Quik Internet Services, Mail Boxes Etc., Athlete's Foot, and General Nutrition Center (GNC). And this is just the tip of the iceberg. Whatever your interest, you can most likely find a franchise to buy.

With a higher success rate, strong business operation systems, and solid marketing plans that often include national advertising, opening a franchise is an option that has a great deal to offer. Its appeal lies in the franchiser's tried-and-true formula for running a business successfully, which will positively impact your success and profits.

For every seven small businesses that fail within the first year of operation, only one is a franchise, reports the Department of Commerce. So why isn't everyone opening franchises? Two reasons: the fees and the necessity to conform. Franchise fees include the initial purchase price, which can be as low as a few hundred dollars or as high as a million dollars (for instance, to start up and launch the granddaddy of all franchises—a McDonald's—will cost you over $1 million). A franchise cost doesn't end with the initial fees—royalties must be paid to the franchise parent company every year as long as you own the business. Some people eventually resent having to pay these royalty fees once their business is strong and they no longer need the constant support and assistance from the parent franchise that they needed when they first opened.

The other reason, besides fees, that causes some people to reject franchise ownership is conformity. Franchises have a set, standard way of operating and doing business, and owners must comply with established rules. "Some independence must be given up," said David Allie, a Mail Boxes Etc. owner. "Franchise owners also need to complete a lot of paperwork, reports, and documentation as a part of the ongoing relationship. Mavericks and free-spirited thinkers might find these requirements reason to go it alone, coupled with the constant fees you'll owe to the parent as long as you're in business."

There are many factors to consider when selecting a franchise. Follow these steps when considering a purchase. First, assess the product or service and determine a location. Explore the franchise—its rules, standards, capital investments, and availability in your region—and investigate its background and financial solvency. Household brands go bankrupt every day, so don't assume, *know* the company's financial position. Be sure to interview several people who own franchises to get a real picture of both the good and the bad about that particular franchise. Additionally, obtain solid accounting and legal advice before you sign any franchising contract.

Be aware that most franchisers will investigate your credit, financial history, and business experience to assess your background and financial strength before they'll agree to sell you a franchise.

A good investigative resource for information on franchises is *220 Best Franchises to Buy,* by the Philip Lief Group and Lynie Arden (Broadway Books, 2000).

Buying an Existing Business

Medical, dental and legal practices, veterinary clinics, chiropractic offices, accounting, architectural and engineering firms, and other professional service businesses, as well as gift stores, restaurants, and the like, are frequently sold when an owner wishes to retire, relocate, or liquidate.

Buying an existing practice or business provides you with an ongoing business that's generating income, with an established clientele and secured location. You can review the business's finance books and examine the overhead and profit margins for the last few years to determine if the asking price is fair. Price is often an arbitrary factor. Figuring out the actual costs of equipment and furniture is only part of it. Most sellers want reimbursement for the goodwill of the established customers, patients, clients. A common mistake is to see a great cash flow and assume it's exactly what you'll bring home if you buy the business.

Dr. Jeff Dieter, owner of Professional Practice Specialists (www.practicesales.com), is a broker who negotiates deals when dentists and chiropractors buy or sell their practices. Dr. Dieter shared some terrific advice about buying a practice or existing business.

"You must assume some business will be lost as a result of the sale," he said. "The best way to minimize this loss is to match your personality and practice techniques to the seller's. The more alike you are, the better the retention of customers will be. A great match might lose only 6% of the business, a poor match will lose 40%. A poor match means the odds are you'll not survive if you purchase the business—the loss of customers, added to your own loan debts and family bills, will sink you.

"To insure that you'll succeed," Dr. Dieter continued, "after selecting a good match, expect a reasonable loss of customers (less than 10% if the match is very good, since this is the style, technique, and operation the customers like and are already buying). Establish a transition period in which the seller and staff stay on (usually three weeks to three months). This creates a more natural flow and keeps customer retention higher. Consider keeping previous staff members on long term, since they are the only people the customer will have a relationship with after the seller is gone," he recommended.

"People assume you can achieve success without buying an existing practice, yet all our research shows that acquiring one along with its cash flow will be an easier road than starting up a whole new business. It's just gotten much harder in recent years for new professionals to open from scratch, build [the practice], survive, and prosper," Dr. Dieter noted. "Student loans, debts, and the needs of supporting a family make starting from scratch and financial survival very difficult, even in the best of situations, such as returning to your hometown, where you know everyone and everyone knows you," he cautioned.

Having had experience with many doctors and their practices and career options myself, I believe Dr. Dieter's advice is quite accurate. Now that schools are producing more professionals then ever before, going it alone has become a more difficult path. So plan and decide carefully.

People achieve only what they aim at.
—HENRY DAVID THOREAU

Working from Home

Today, 53% of all small businesses are run from home.

I love working from home. I sure don't miss the 90-minute, parking-lot-traffic-crawl commute I used to make. These days I sit in my sweats, answering emails or conducting a radio phone interview, grateful that radio is *not* a visual medium. I'm not alone in my enjoyment of working from home. Twenty-seven million Americans like working from home, too. The rent is cheap, and the ease and flexibility make it very appealing.

Mary Ann Konis had never been employed. A mother of two, she home-schooled her son and daughter until they entered middle school. She wasn't looking to start a business six years ago, but she stumbled upon a product that captured her interest and enthusiasm. Preserving her family's photos and immortalizing their cherished times became a passion after she was introduced to a new scrapbooking product line produced by Creative Memories. She enjoyed the product and loved sharing scrapbooking ideas with others. She became a consultant (at a cost of less than $200) to take advantage of the discount she received on the products, a move that launched her home-based business. Today, Mary Ann is a successful businesswoman who manages and teaches other consultants and conducts some seminars on scrapbooking. She operates her entire business from her home.

Mary Ann shared what many home-based business owners know—the hardest thing about running a home-based business is to *not* work all the time. In the excitement of living your passion, business owners say, those start-up years may begin part-time, but they can quickly evolve into sixty-, seventy-, or even eighty-hour weeks. "Setting up regular business hours while still keeping some flexibility is the key," Mary Ann advised. Many other business owners said this is a good way to protect family time and refrain from making every waking hour, seven days a week, your business time.

Mary Ann pointed out, "I train a lot of new home-based businesspeople. The biggest reason that I see for failure is that people are not committed to doing the hard work. They must become businesspeople—it's the essential ingredient for success. They need to learn how to control costs and achieve a profit."

Many businesses fail because they didn't make any profit, or not enough to survive. So a big question in your research and planning is this: How much profit can and will you honestly make?

Another stumbling block to success for home businesses is created when business owners do not completely review the pros and cons of working from home. If you are a parent, I suggest you read Azriela Jaffe's book, *Honey, I Want to Start My Own Business* (HarperBusiness, 1996). It's an excellent resource on the actual steps to consider, particularly if you are considering working from home. Jaffe says you must set up business rules to help you succeed. Here are some initial questions she suggests you ask yourself: How will my home business suit my marriage and family? What are the challenges and rewards of running the business from my home? What will the rules need to be to protect both my family and my work time? Should I move or operate the business elsewhere?

How to Start a Business While You Still Work Full-time

One way to guarantee job security is to become your own boss and open a business. Franchises, storefront operations, home-based businesses, product sales, professional practices, and consulting are all possible ways to become an entrepreneur. Thousands of people are doing it. But not everyone has the luxury of pursuing their passionate dreams by just quitting and "going for it," and some may not want to. Some prefer to test the waters of self-employment gradually, investing small amounts of time and money into a hobby, network marketing opportunity, or entrepreneurial brainstorm, nurturing this seed into a flower before cutting off their main source of income.

You must have realistic expectations. Since you are still working, you'll need to use your time wisely. Plan a schedule to work the business and also begin to develop good marketing materials. About 90% of your time will be spent looking for and trying to attract customers. Collect ideas from colleagues, friends, and other businesses that might be adapted to work for you. Read books on sales, marketing, direct mail, and advertising. Above all, test for results before you invest large sums of money in any marketing endeavor. A lot will change during your first year of operation. Consider printing smaller quantities or using the excellent predesigned papers available.

Eventually you'll need to decide when to quit and try to run your venture full-time. "The most stressful time usually comes at a stage when the part-time business has become so successful that it demands more hours and brings in just enough money to tempt you to quit your day job," said Azriela Jaffe. "You believe that if you gave your fledgling business your full-time commitment, you could equal or exceed the salary you are bringing in now."

Before you quit, I recommend you have six months of income saved to meet your financial obligations without any income from your self-employment venture. Remember, underfinancing typically leads to failure. Jaffe added, "Plan out and purchase insurance benefits your family might need if you quit your job. Be ready for no more days off or sick leave—since you (and your work) are the business. Part-time self-employment may be a whole lot more fun, when you still have a day job that supports you. On the other hand, once you quit your job, you may never look back."

Turn a Hobby into a Career

Many business owners confess to having a hobby that eventually turned into a career. I started my seminar business as a hobby. I know many writers who began working on their craft at nights or on weekends, eventually doing some freelance articles that led to a whole new career. Graphic designers, event planners, fundraisers, photographers, and Web designers—many people started out by either volunteering or just doing the work for fun or a few extra dollars.

Eventually, everyone must decide to get serious about making an avocation a true career. Although there are many paths one can follow, finances often present the greatest obstacle to making the switch. The best way to move along is to plan out your transition. First, moonlight and learn on somebody else's dime. Use spare time to learn and perfect your interest. Read books on business, take classes, and get training so that you can develop a new "paying" career. Even five hours a week can be a start on learning new skills and making money using them.

Few wishes come true by themselves. Carefully develop an action plan, outlining and defining the steps you'll need to take to make a living from your hobby. If it's a new business, you'll need a plan detailing the product, service, or idea, who the potential buyers and competitors are, sales and marketing options, pricing, revenue projections, and so on. Network and learn from others who have succeeded so you can benefit from their trials and errors. As your business grows, you'll need to get more help at home, either by dividing up chores with other family members or by hiring someone to do some things (such as housecleaning or yardwork) for you.

Many people's stores and businesses were born from pursuing hobbies or avocations. The key is that your hobby is something you enjoy and believe you'd like to do every day. Don't underestimate your own happiness quotient as you make your career decisions. When you are working at something you love, it can enrich your whole life, making everyone around you happier. But eventually you have to take some risks, overcome your fear, and just do it. The key to moving the hobby forward is to predetermine exactly how much time, energy, and effort you can and will put into it. Then *plan, plan, plan.* Implement gradually, and your action steps will eventually enable you to work at the career of your dreams.

Where Does the Start-up Money Come From?

Most people finance their business from their own resources. Savings, severance packages, retirement incomes, borrowed family money, inheritances—these usually fund the venture. Of course, there are some unique stories. One woman sued a company for sexual harassment and wrongful dismissal. She knew she'd never get hired again once insiders heard of the lawsuit, so she used her large settlement to set up her own recruitment company and has prospered ever since. Another man won some money in Las Vegas and used it to launch his own car detailing business, which became so successful that it now has numerous locations and has made him quite wealthy in the process.

There are others like Rich Leo and Mark Tranter, who ran an executive recruiting company and launched their own business—a national online recruiting firm. They wrote an extensive business plan and presented it successfully to venture capitalists to obtain funding for their idea. Neither got paid during the tight months of the start-up year. They lived off personal savings, since the capitalists' funding covered operations costs but not their own salaries as founders.

CEO Debbie Coleman is an expert at building companies (she's done it six times, quite successfully). She offered sage advice for those who need investors to make their dream come true. The key to attracting investors is to build a working model. Launch the company and develop the product, but seek out investors in waves. The first influx of money gets you going—then you work hard, show demand, and demonstrate that the product or service is initially successful.

She recommended you hit a milestone of a certain level of achievement and then go to investors for more money. You should repeat this pattern—using the new funds to reach the next milestone—a build-and-grow, build-and-grow approach. This strategy works because at each milestone you are proving the company's success and potential, making it easier to attract investors. Coleman is doing that now, and her current company will most likely hit $100 million within the year.

"The other piece you need to make this work is you must hire great talent," she added. "Smart people with experience in their fields, be it sales, distribution, accounting, whatever—the team of people and their desire to win are all essential to continue to succeed and grow and attract investors' dollars."

As you consider the possibility of opening your own business, you must determine how much money you'll need not only for the business start-up, but to pay your own bills. A key error is to think you'll make a big salary quickly. It typically takes two to three years before a new business generates enough funds to cover operation expenses and is able to pay you a salary.

Running the Business

To run your business successfully, you must master a few basics. The first and foremost task is to learn accounting! You must understand debt, credits, and cash flow and have a grip on standard business operating procedures. You'll need good records—QuickBooks, an accounting software program by Intuit, is a good one to consider. You'll be able to create and track invoices, sales, and expenses and even do your taxes with it.

You'll need to get a business license, both state and local. You'll need to understand the rules and pay numerous taxes. It's best to go to an accountant and learn all these basics, so you'll be sure you're paying all your taxes on a timely basis. Set up a separate bank account to deposit your tax money into each month, and make sure you save the dollars you'll need to cover all taxes (state, federal, and payroll). These can be quite high, so be sure to get good financial advice in the beginning and as needed once you are operating.

The next thing is to learn marketing skills, since obtaining clients or customers is a key factor in your success. Determine exactly how much money you can designate to marketing at the start and then on an ongoing basis. Business cards, websites, and brochures are all important, but your business will change and grow a lot in the first year or two, so keep print jobs small—

additions and changes will be easier to make. Sometimes things outside your control can force you to reprint your materials. Many a business owner has gotten stuck with this costly prospect because the phone company changed her area code, making materials obsolete in a short time. So always plan for unexpected marketing costs and have some funds available to cover them.

The best way to acquire marketing skills is to read books and use the information applicable to your business. Bookstores and libraries are full of business books, so make time to read at least two books per month to advance your business operator education. Also, seek advice from others on what marketing tricks worked for them and what wasn't worth the money.

It's wise to take a class or two and be sure you have the necessary computer skills to run a business. Time management and business operations courses can also be helpful. Learn everything necessary, as your primary job is now "business owner," first and foremost above whatever technical skill or craft your business entails.

Now It's Your Turn

Can anybody make it? The world is full of success stories that say this statement is absolutely true.

Consider Marion Luna Brem. Battling cervical and breast cancer and wearing a wig to hide the effects of chemotherapy, this thirty-two-year-old Hispanic woman saw her marriage collapse, leaving her with two sons to raise. She had staggering medical bills and very little work experience, and she desperately needed a job. In 1984, few women worked in the field of car sales, and sixteen dealers told her no before she found an employer willing to give her a try. One year later, still working at that car dealership, she was named "Salesperson of the Year." Five years later she opened her own dealership, followed by another. Today she oversees 120 employees running her Love Chrysler business and generates annual revenues of $45 million. At age forty-eight, Brem seems a bit dazed by her own story, as reported in *USA Today*. "I look back on it in awe," she was quoted as saying.

Anyone can achieve this kind of success; it's just a matter of motivation. You may want something that equals or surpasses Brem's achievements. Your desires might be less lofty in magnitude but still important to you.

Let's evaluate your options for opening a business. To review what's already been stated, select your new passion carefully. There's a mountain of options to choose from when you consider what kind of business to open, so do your research. Look at the business's overall potential, evaluating the types of customers as well as the start-up and operational costs. Examine your potential competitors. Visit their organizations, review their marketing and sales materials, and get a list of their prices or fees. Interview and learn from people who already operate the type of business you want to pursue. If you don't have a burning passion for the industry, keep looking.

Make a complete list of the start-up expenses, equipment purchases, office furniture, printing expenses, marketing materials, and so forth. Now add in 15% extra, because new business owners usually underestimate true costs. Collect and review marketing materials from competitors' businesses, noting services and fees for each. Summarize the market research and trends that support opening this business. List information obtained from interviewing no fewer than five successful business owners, including business pros, cons, market conditions, competition, and the long-term picture. Analyze your interview information and note what makes this potential business succeed, according to the owners you spoke with. Record possible business pitfalls you've heard of or noticed. To conclude, list all reasons to select this business, then create the action steps and plan to move forward.

You can spend your whole life waiting and hoping for opportunity to knock. Yet only you can knock on the door that leads to your own destiny. Knowing that opportunity lies inside each of us will help you to answer that knock and achieve all you are capable of. Never sell yourself short. Anything anyone else has done, you can probably do as well, or even better!

CHAPTER 6

Getting Paid Well for What You Do

I'm a great believer in luck. I find the harder
I work, the more I have of it.
—THOMAS JEFFERSON, THIRD PRESIDENT
OF THE UNITED STATES

No one is overpaid. If someone wants to pay you, whatever it is he or she wants to pay you, you're worth it. Baseball star Alex Rodriguez got a contract for $252,000,000—yes, *million*—obviously, some people (with big bucks) felt he was worth it.

"You've got to pay for the talent," said one Fortune 500 CEO. "I'm not gonna quibble over a few thousand dollars. Once I decide the person I want to hire can contribute the results I need, I know I have to have him on *my* team. Then I'll pay whatever it takes to get him."

"Take the job that pays you the most," recommended Jim Medzegian, who sits on the board of trustees of Renton Technical College and is a former senior executive at the Boeing Company. "All future raises and bonuses are calculated on what your base is when you begin."

The biggest financial increases come from changing jobs—especially if you change jobs *and* receive a promotion at the same time. We'll address the salary negotiation process in this chapter.

To begin, you must determine and acknowledge your true market value. You must expect to be paid well for your contributions. Your attitude and assumptions will directly impact the outcome of any financial negotiations you undertake.

Salary Negotiations

Men and women approach salary negotiations quite differently. If I were to call a man and a woman with similar backgrounds and offer them the same job, typically the end result would be amazingly different. I've confirmed this observation over the years with clients and many employers. Women generally *accept* the offer that is presented. Men tend to negotiate and ask for more.

Allen was a controller who did his homework prior to negotiating his salary with his new boss. He knew the salary range typically paid by employers in this field and thought through why the hiring manager wanted to hire him. Using these factors and his knowledge of the field, this client put together a Hiring Chart (see page 106) that outlined the department and job needs, as well as his past contributions in those areas.

Additionally, Allen called the personnel department for the details of the benefits package. He rehearsed his negotiations to be comfortable asking for more and pointing out why he was worth that investment. He arrived at the negotiations meeting armed with tools and a strategy to persuade this employer to pay more.

The offer started at $63,000, but Allen negotiated and obtained a base salary of $71,000. That's $8,000 more, a *12% increase,* to start. All bonuses and future raises are paid off that starting base. Had Allen accepted the initial offer, his 20% bonus would have been $12,600. But because he successfully negotiated a higher base salary, his first year's 20% bonus would be $14,200. He's ahead of his peers' base salary and will thus receive bigger raises and bonuses throughout his tenure with this company.

That's an important fact to remember. Those who try to ne-

HIRING CHART	
Needs	**Contributions**
CPA	13 years in the accounting field, 5 as a controller for a midsize company
Computer Network Systems	LAN expertise and programming capability. Developed corporate network and integrated entire system. Provided technical support to all departments. Implemented computerized GL system, inventory and billing system. Eliminated two full-time staff positions as a result while increasing overall productivity.
Reengineering	Team leader of company's entire reengineering efforts. Costs decreased by 7%, productivity enhancements increased by 30%.
Vendor/Negotiations	Negotiated over 400+ contracts, obtaining better prices, discounts, and terms. Savings surpasses $100,000.
Bank Relations	Coordinated cash management and negotiated loans and lines of credit on cyclical business to maintain strong cash flow.

gotiate salary usually succeed. Most often, the only difference is they *asked* and you didn't.

Why Women Are Still Paid Less Than Men

The Annual Working Women salary survey, published by *Working Women* magazine, and other recent labor studies show women are still paid 23% *less* than men. Women tend to devalue themselves as workers and accept whatever's offered. They aren't as aggressive as men in their salary negotiations. Women wrote to me after reading my book on interviewing techniques (*60 Seconds & You're Hired!*) and told me that they had never negotiated salary before. They reported that when they did use the salary negotiation techniques I outlined in my book, they surprised themselves by getting better offers. One client, Martha, was determined to ask for a higher salary after receiving a job offer. She discussed it with her prospective employer, telling her she thought the offer was a bit low. The employer immediately offered $3,000 more, plus a $2,000 signing bonus. Her new boss later told her she got really worried when Martha didn't accept the offer right away. So, the boss put together the best package she could. She really wanted to hire Martha. "Wow! I'd never have believed I could do this, but it's sure gonna be fun spending all that extra money," Martha told me.

The first rule of salary negotiations is—*try*. In minutes, you can find yourself thousand of dollars richer. (There's a complete formula for success that I'll outline a little later in this chapter.) Use documentation and persuasive arguments. There's psychology and human behavior at play here that you need to recognize. Fact: Once the employer decides "you are the one," he ends the *selection* process and moves to the *recruiting* process. He begins to sell you on the job and the company. He worries you won't take the job. His panic increases. He *wants you*. And he wants to *get* what he wants. *Whatever it takes!* There lies the secret power of negotiation: waiting until an employer wants you, *you*, and *only you*. That's when the employer is most willing to pay more to get you. This is why it's important to avoid all salary conversations until the job offer has been made.

Determine Your Competitive Salary Worth

Early in your job search, when you respond to want ads that state "send salary history" or encounter salary information requests on job application forms, be careful. This is where job hunters make critical errors.

In a survey I conducted of six hundred hiring managers nationwide, I found that 24% requested salary history as a part of their hiring process, most specifically in their want ads. Personnel managers and top executives all told us the same thing: Salary histories are used to *screen people out and to get a true estimation of the real level of job duties performed.* That means salary information is used to *eliminate* you. Therefore our strategy is this: Simply don't mention salary in your cover letter at all.

Sometimes employers' ads state, "Only those sending salary histories will be considered." Okay—our approach is to not tell them what you made. So instead try this technique, which has been highly effective for my clients.

Cite an appropriate source, such as your trade association or a national salary survey, and state: "According to the American Hotel and Motel Association, the average salary for assistant manager at a medium-size hotel ranges from $50,000 to $80,000, and I'd expect to be paid in that range." This approach leaves the door open to future negotiation and puts you within a highly respected industry guideline. Additionally, you often don't know if a company pays below or above the average. So using a wide—but factual—range gives you a good playing field to negotiate with later. *Remember this fact: The first person to mention money* loses.

In my experience with clients and in conversations I've had with employers, the salary range has worked as a good alternative to the demand for a salary history. Still, the best option, whenever possible, is to mention nothing. Salary information eliminates those whose salaries are too high and, more commonly, those whose salaries are *too low.*

Applications are legal documents—never lie on them. Any false statement (such as fudging on your salary) could result in termination should the lie be uncovered later. *Leave blank* the line requesting salary earned at your old job. Remember, our strategy to obtain the highest salary possible is to never mention salary before the employer does. Our goal is to obtain the highest salary possible for you. Waiting until the employer offers a salary or salary range gives you the upper hand and a position of strength to deal from.

A Fatal Mistake to Avoid

The interview is where most job candidates make fatal and unfixable salary mistakes. Number one: They reveal their former salary. Jeffrey, an engineer with a few years' experience, interviewed for a job he really wanted. He'd been laid off from his previous job and was eager to get to work again. During the interview, the employer asked: "What were you making at the old company?" "$44,000," he told them. Not surprisingly, he was offered the job at $45,000.

He called to discuss his situation with me. He was seeking an offer of $50,000 and had just learned that the salary scale ranged from $43,000 to $55,000. Realizing his mistake, Jeffrey said, "I'm dead in the water, aren't I, since I told them my old salary?"

I replied, "Pretty much, yes. You're not working, their offer is equivalent to your old job, and they know it. You can try to negotiate, but now that the personnel department is involved, it'll be hard—if not impossible—to overcome now that they know exactly what you were making."

Jeffrey then asked, "Can I fake it—bluff? Hint that I have another offer?"

"I don't advise it," I told him. "Poker is one thing, but this is your future, and if they say, 'Forget it,' you've lost out on a real job. If you are willing to spend more weeks searching and feel this company's not great, you can always walk away. So my question to you, Jeffrey, is—is it okay to not take this job and wait for another?"

"No," he concluded. "There's a lot I can learn here. This is a good base salary, and I do like the company. I guess I just learned a very expensive lesson about salary negotiation, didn't I?"

The moral of the story: Never mention your old salary. Ever.

Who Can Negotiate for a Higher Salary?

The more years of experience and specific skills you acquire, the more leverage you have to negotiate salary. It's a fairly common practice for both midcareer and senior executives to open the door and negotiate a higher salary with the techniques I've outlined. But what about those just starting out on a new career path or at the lower end of the pay scale? These techniques work, whether you seek to make $15,000 or $50 more. Many clients starting out in new careers have successfully negotiated higher starting salaries. In the early years of your career, the most important consideration must be seeking out good opportunities to learn from a good manager, as well as on the job. Sometimes employers balk at offering you more, but if you think it's a good job, you should accept it. If you do try to negotiate, here's the advice I typically offer clients with less than five years of experience: Keep your salary requests small. If you ask for $50–$100 more per month, this is a small enough amount, and the probability is that the employer will say yes. Beginning engineers, MBAs, computer programmers, and nurses might be able to negotiate higher salaries right out of college, owing to the demand for their skills. I encourage these people to get a realistic number based on other classmates' offers, so they'll know what to ask for during negotiations.

Career changers don't have to start at the bottom. Don't overlook your hidden assets. Peg left her job as a hospital administrator to enter the graphic arts field. Once she'd completed all the new training and had a year of experience, she began job hunting. She landed a prime position—director of communications at a college—that actually paid more than her old hospital job did. She oversaw all the graphic designers and landed the job by selling the old management skills she'd acquired in her position as a hospital administrator. She discussed her hiring and staffing skills, project management expertise, extensive customer service skills, budget management strengths—all relevant to performing the new job. Her transferable skills were a big plus and helped soften her minimal graphic arts experience.

Transferable skills—mention them often, as they often result in obtaining a higher salary even when you're entering an entirely new career, industry, or field.

The Nine Secrets for Salary Negotiation Success

1. Research and Determine Your True Market Value
All salary negotiations must be based on facts, not assumptions. This step—often the most difficult—is essential for success. You must know what is a fair price for your services. Search the Internet, business magazines, and association websites and journals to locate the salary surveys and data you'll need.

2. Effectively Communicate Your Value
Use the interview as a time to continuously reaffirm your value to the employer. Use proven examples from your past to demonstrate how you can be a key contributor. This focus on how you'll meet the employer's needs entices him or her to want you more.

3. Never Mention Salary First

In this power game, you tip your hand if you volunteer your salary expectation before the employer tells you the range or exact figure the job pays. You should always speak in ranges, never exact figures. Employers equate salary with level of duties and can dismiss you because your "lower salary" means you weren't performing skills at the level they seek—even if you were. So refrain from ever mentioning a figure.

4. Never Tell an Employer Your Old Salary

This gives you the best leverage when it's time to negotiate. If you do tell the employer, you will usually live to regret it. One national sales manager who hadn't looked for a job in eighteen years took a W-2 to her first interview after her layoff. She "proved" she was well paid. Too bad the new company's manager discounted her as a high-level candidate—her figure on the W-2 ($102,000) was significantly lower than his range so he rationalized that she was not as good as she claimed based on what she was paid before.

5. Quantify Your Worth

Once the offer is made, ask the employer why you were selected. Listen closely, then center your salary demand arguments on what you're told and everything else you've learned in the interview. Focus continuously on how effectively you'll meet the employer's needs and excel at the job. Reassure her you'll be up to speed and productive quickly, stressing that in a short time you'll be a contributor. Resell her on exactly why she offered you the job in the first place. Using the Hiring Chart (see page 106) can be a powerful way to persuade the employer. The interviewer may need to go to a higher authority for approval of your request for a higher salary. This chart provides solid evidence and validates your persuasive arguments when it's passed on to upper management.

6. Use a Win-Win Approach

Realistic expectations and the willingness to "settle" or "compromise" allow both parties to end negotiations happy. Showing you'll come down a little if the employer goes up a little can often be the key to success, as it allows both parties—you and the employer—to walk away feeling as though each has won.

7. Know Your Bottom Line

Some organizations will negotiate salary. The higher your position, the more likely it is that salary will be negotiated. Other employers may predetermine the dollars they can spend to have a job done and will not (and in most cases don't have the budget to) pay more, no matter how good you are. City, state, federal, and many nonprofit jobs often have a pay scale that indexes job experience into a salary, with little more than a $1,000–$2,000 leeway.

Your decision must take into account the whole picture. Company atmosphere, growth potential, stress level (and lack of), coworkers, training options, commute time, flexible hours, benefits, perks such as cars or free day care—all must be considered as you make your decision. You know what is most important to you—perhaps a few extra dollars weighed against a two-hour commute every day isn't worth it.

Predetermine the lowest offer you'll accept and be willing to pass on lower salaries. Sometimes a person's financial situation forces him to accept the first job offered. Then it's not long before he's back trying to plan out a way to get a promotion, raise, or new (better-paying) job. Many of my clients turned down low offers and in just a few weeks had the right—and better-paying—job come along.

8. Never Bluff

Ultimatums can result in offers being withdrawn. Don't lie. Never fib or bluff an employer. "I have other offers" might get the response, "So take them." Unless the offer is concrete and real, don't go down this road.

9. Promises Are Not Guarantees

Many employers have both selective memories and ever-changing budgets. Promises of future bonuses and raises often disappear once you're on the job. The promise of a bonus after six months is negated when a companywide letter saying "No bonuses this year" arrives in month three, leaving you with few options. Negotiate hard to get the money, benefits, and perks *up front*. Then get it in writing. You can ask the employer for this letter of employment or write it yourself and have the employer countersign it. It's a simple statement of facts that guarantees exactly what all parties agreed to.

Negotiating Tips to Get the Perks You Want

Today, companies worried about retaining talent are beefing up their benefits packages. Stock options and the lure of getting rich caused major corporate defections in the last few years, forcing companies to offer more attractive perks to current and new workers. These perks totally impact a person's decision to accept or decline a job. The number one thing people want when moving to a new employer is more vacation, especially if only a week is offered. Full employer-paid medical coverage is a close second, followed by signing bonuses. Then, of course, there are the extras like computers (including laptops), pagers, cell phones, data organizers, and so on, all billed to the company. And when relocating, people want all expenses covered plus an extra bonus for the hassle of moving.

A lucky percentage of people are offered stock options or profit sharing. The high-tech industry has used stock options as a lure to get workers to put in long hours (commonly seventy to eighty per week) for lesser salaries, affirming stock options as a "bonus" with the seductive incentive that the options will pay off and make workers rich, rich, rich—or so the hype goes. And people did get rich. "Microsoft millionaires" literally took over the Seattle housing market simply by selling more stock options to outbid anyone on the houses they wanted, running up home prices exorbitantly. Cash from options bought luxury cars, in multiple colors, for Silicon Valley techies rolling in stock option dollars. Then the market crashed and many people's options became worth less and less—in some cases, worth absolutely nothing.

It's important to remember that stock options are not a guarantee of anything. They can be a very nice payoff if you are lucky and smart about how you negotiate them. The key is to ask for shorter vesting times and, if possible, also demand that they become fully vested immediately in the event of a merger or buyout. Additionally, try to extend the length of time you need to exercise your stock options upon leaving an employer. In the case of my client Connie, her options had the typical ninety-day exercise clause in them. When her wireless company relocated, she lost her job and had to exercise (use) the options, buying and selling the stock within ninety-days of her departure. Since this was a time when the company's stock was low, her options were worth only $10,000. Had she had a clause that allowed her a longer period—say, one year—she would have had the option to wait and see if the stock price rebounded and improved before she had to sell.

Therefore, when negotiating stock options, ask for the following:
1. Shorter vesting period.
2. Immediate vesting upon a merger or buyout.
3. An extended period of time, upon departure from company, before being required to exercise the options.

The first rule to negotiating perks is to know what you want. Create a dream list of extras an employer could provide, with the top priority first. Many employers recognize individual needs and may ask you what you'd like. Knowing you value subsidized day care or a bigger car allowance serves you well in getting exactly what you want.

Don't be afraid to try. This means you—yes, *you*. Whether you are a man or a woman, unemployed or working, *ask*. Go on, test the waters. See if there is room for more. It won't hurt to mention these things would really sell you on the company as you are negotiating a job offer. You won't get more if you don't ask.

Do your homework. Evaluate the company's entire benefit plan. What about vacation time, flexible hours, tuition reimbursement, fewer hours, days off, relocation expenses, stock options, company car, expense accounts, bonuses? Know exactly what is being offered. Look closely at the medical plan. What kind of coverage is provided? What deductibles does the plan include? Who pays for dependents? If you pay, what will that cost be? My clients have argued successfully for a higher salary to compensate for switching medical plans where the old employer covered the entire family and the new one covers just the employee. Predetermine which benefits are important to you and ask for them. Or suggest a higher base salary to compensate if the requested perk can't be given.

Vacations and days off can often be negotiated. If you had four weeks' vacation from your last boss (with ten years of service), it is unlikely the new company will give you four weeks. Be reasonable, but do inquire and state what you want. Numerous employers respond by offering an additional week or two or a few paid personal days if that was what you requested.

Think through this negotiation interview, visualizing a successful outcome. Then ask a friend to role-play the interview. Defend why you are worth the company upping its offer. Listen to the feedback—did you convince him or her? This preparation will decrease your anxiety and increase your confidence. You can point out competitors' policies. Most companies know they can't retain good people if their perks fall too far behind the competition's. Be sure to mention other policies or benefits that particularly appeal to you and ask if they can be met and/or offered.

Use a Letter of Employment

Solidify your hard-earned salary negotiations in a written document. Here's an example:

CONFIDENTIAL

Dear (employer):

I'm happy to accept your position as your new psychologist. We have agreed to the following terms:

Salary: $75,000

Hours: Mon.–Thurs. 8–5, plus first and third Thursday facilitate group session from 6:00 to 8:00 P.M. Fridays—no clients, work from home. (one-hour lunch on Mon.–Thurs.)

Vacations: 1 day per month

Sick: 1 day per month

Parking: reimbursed by the company

Benefits: Medical (including family coverage at $100/month); 401(k), life and disability as company offers

Starting Date: June 7

I look forward to a long and successful working relationship. This letter of understanding serves as a binding agreement between Christine Thompson and Southhill Mental Health Center and its representative, Director Jonathan Murphy.

| Christine Thompson | Date | Jonathan Murphy | Date |
| Psychologist | | Director | |

Four Keys to Successful Salary Negotiations

1. Never mention $$$ first.
2. Continuously sell yourself and reiterate your value.
3. Ask a fair price.
4. Evaluate the whole offer against your long-term goals and objectives.

Employment letters are necessary, and definitely so whenever you deviate from the standard company plan. In the employment letter sample, the new employee negotiated reimbursed parking (a $120 savings per month). When she got her first check, it was not included. Without this letter of agreement she would have lost that extra, promised benefit. It seems her new boss didn't recall ever agreeing to the parking subsidy. A written letter eliminates a lot of potential misunderstandings down the line and, in this case, got her free parking, for a $1,440 annual savings.

Multiple Job Offers— When the Whole World Wants *You*

Occasionally, a client is fortunate to have a job offer from one employer and can actually create a bidding war by bringing in another employer. One client I had received one offer and wanted to try to motivate another, more desirable employer to also make an offer. This is tricky, as there are numerous factors outside your control. First, go to the second employer and say honestly and politely, "I've got a firm offer I need to decide on. I'm still very interested in your job. Can you tell me whether I'm still in the running as a top candidate, since this information could influence my decision?" Three answers can come forth. "No"—so now you aren't betting on a dream. "We haven't decided"—ask for a timeline, but don't force the employer to meet your scheduled deadline. You may have to accept the first offer and play along with this other employer if he or she is weeks away from a choice. There is always the option of quitting a job a few weeks after you start it to go to a better position if you get a later offer. This action won't win friends, but it does happen. The third option, "Yes, you are our top candidate," requires you to again nail down the employer's timeline. He or she may counter immediately with an offer. By asking, you'll be making your decision based on facts—not on hopes, hunches, or maybes.

One client, Lee, a computer systems analyst, had three offers. All had various components. One required relocation. I had him outline each offer by salary and benefits, noting the pluses and minuses of each company. This cleared up exactly what he was comparing. Since a move was involved, he also took his wife's preferences into consideration. She agreed to move only if the money was worth it.

When Lee had trouble deciding, I had him go see each employer again. These visits were insightful, as he was able to learn more about the individual culture of each company. After that final stop, he felt the move to California was the best offer. He decided the move would indeed be worth it once the company agreed to add another $10,000 for relocation and to help him with the sale and purchase of his home.

If you are in a similar boat, visit each employer again. Where would you be able to use your talents the best? Your potential happiness is the barometer in your decision-making process. Money does not always buy happiness. Make your selection after some soul-searching, careful thought, and reflection.

Conclusion

Salary negotiations are an important career management strategy you must use any time you leave one employer and join another. Quitting your job and moving on to a new employer is how most people accomplish the largest salary jumps.

Today, many of my clients are living fuller, richer lives because they successfully used salary negotiations to obtain their true value. Scott left Boeing when he failed to get a deserved promotion. His old salary was $56,000 (including bonuses). His new job started at $72,000 *plus* bonuses. Four years and two promotions later, he's making well over six figures. His wife doesn't work and cares for their sons in a beautiful new 3,000-square-foot home—their lifestyle is a product of his decision to move on and get paid in full for the value he contributed to an organization.

Lauren left her full-time employer and went to work as a part-time controller for a new company. She negotiated her true worth and is now making almost exactly what she made at her old job, working ten hours less per week. Another client doubled his salary when he left the nonprofit world and took a corporate job. So many of my clients are making more money. Why? They negotiated better salaries and benefits for themselves and in a few short minutes made themselves a great deal richer. So if you want to get paid the most money possible to do your job—negotiate!

PART 3
Staying Put

With $200 in my pocketbook, Wynonna,
Ashley, and I moved to Nashville and after a
few years became an "overnight" success in
the music industry. But throughout the
material and outward success, I also made
the choice to pursue personal excellence.
That is what truly satisfies the soul, and no
amount of money or power can fill that
void. Nobody is born with their destiny
stamped on their foreheads. You have the
opportunity to change your life at any
moment. If you know in your heart that
you have done your absolute best and
acknowledge the talents and gifts that you
have been blessed with, your life will find
its own rewards.

—NAOMI JUDD

CHAPTER 7

CEOs and Top Executives Reveal How to Get Promoted

There is no use in trying to help people who do not help themselves, for you cannot push anyone up a ladder unless they are willing to climb by themselves.

—ANDREW CARNEGIE

One of our country's top CEOs, who runs a national retail store chain, began her career as a secretary. She's sure had a lot of promotions since then.

Another CEO began as a teacher. Another started out as a mechanic. Someone else said he began as a sales rep. No one started out at the top. All the executives in our survey started at the bottom somewhere. These people did a lot right, made mistakes, learned from them, and got noticed. They ultimately produced results, and today they're the executives looking down the ranks, deciding if you'll get the promotion or if someone else should.

If you are reading this chapter, you've already thought through how a promotion would affect your life. In earlier chapters, we explored the impacts of a new promotion—the stress, increased workload, drain on your family time, and so on. You've come here because you want more challenge, more money—you want to shape your company's or organization's outcomes.

Survey Results

You want to learn the best ways to get promoted. I could have asked hiring or middle-level managers for their advice. In fact, I have asked them many times in the past, and I got good insight into how to move up a level. But the workplace is changing so fast, I realized that to truly paint a picture of the traits and behaviors necessary to move up and build your career, I needed to ask the right people, the ones who sit at the top. So that's exactly what I did.

I surveyed many top executives for this book—the people who run their organizations. I got input from many industry leaders, from CEOs of Fortune 500 companies to nonprofit directors at associations or charities. Those seventy-eight who completed the comprehensive survey were CEOs, presidents, general managers, or executive directors—the top guns, the big cheeses, the people who *know.*

In their surveys, our top executives offered strategic advice, published here for the first time, to help you get promoted no matter what level you're at or how big your organization is. First and foremost, the executives said that *promotable people are good at what they do and achieve results.* General Manager Mike Lowe recommended you "perform to the best of your abilities," a statement echoed by many top executives. Rising stars demonstrate initiative. This means you must take the time to learn and become very knowledgeable in your field of expertise. A major conclusion of our survey was that employees need *more* than technical competence to get promoted. Our executives were

> Promotable people are good at
> what they do and produce results.

very clear about that, stating unanimously that you need to be
more than just "good at the job."

We asked several questions to get specific advice. Top executives told us in detail what impresses them and what characteristics one must develop to get promoted. Many wrote extensive
accounts of what they see, think, and need from potential employees.

I compiled traits and skills that, according to our surveyed
CEOs and top executives, you need to have to get promoted and
rise in your organization. They are: creative problem solving; integrity, honesty, and hard work; the ability to achieve results, self-
start, and show initiative; a positive outlook and attitude; and
good networking skills.

Company president Kiama Taylor summed it up nicely: "Un-
derpromise, overdeliver. Whatever you say you will do—do it, so
that you are a person of integrity and your word means something. Don't make excuses—the world is swirling with baloney!
Take responsibility, and instead of focusing on why a mistake
wasn't your fault—focus on what can be done to either solve the
problem or create effective damage control."

Yvonne La-Garde, CEO of Lifelinks Inc., clearly stated what
many other top executives echoed. "I'm impressed by hard work
and honesty," she said.

Executive Director Marcia Holland Risch summarized her
opinions and those of others. "Be willing to go the extra mile,"
she said. "Be able to find creative solutions to identified problems, to ask probing questions designed to find solutions, and to
take good care of the people around you. Expressing apprecia-
tion and the ability to admit a mistake and move on to solutions,
with no whining, are key."

One CEO wrote, "Actions speak louder than words. Don't

tell me—show me. Speak up if you think something can be done better." Another CEO advised, "We need people who think ahead and are willing to try something that may be new and different or a bit beyond their immediate skill level."

They pointed out the need for employees to really think about improving the company, then follow through by doing the things necessary to benefit their company, division, or department. You'll help your own career in the process, but your focus will be on the big picture and producing key results that make a difference. Many top executives noted that people often just concentrate on improving their own careers. True rising stars are smart enough to focus on improving the company—in doing so, they get noticed, appreciated, and continuously promoted.

One common thing these executives seemed to hate—people who lie, whine, or blame others. I was surprised by how many commented about this. They abhor excuses. The CEO of a large manufacturing company said, "Come to me or your boss and admit something isn't working, don't just gossip about it. Above all else, don't lie to me—ever." Many noted that gossiping was toxic to success.

Technical Competence and More

Every top executive we surveyed said that job competence alone was not enough to get a promotion. This means you must be competent at what you do, *plus* you need to do several other things if you want to be selected by upper management to move up. Almost every one of our top executives mentioned one key factor that will get you noticed and impress top management—"producing results." It's *the factor* that influences decision makers.

Ann Salamone, chief of operations for Enterprise Development Corporation, said, "You must product results. All other traits, such as being a team player, continuously improving, being a problem solver, strategic thinker, and being tenacious, all add up to that number one thing—*producing results.*" This seems to be the criterion for every top executive! Examine yourself. *Do you get results?* No matter what job you have, you must be able to produce the desired or needed results if you want to get yourself noticed and slated for a move up.

Our top executives listed these descriptions as characteristics of rising stars (in order of importance). First, "produce results." Second, "be a team player." Next, "be a problem solver." Then, "be a strategic thinker." "Continuously improving oneself and the job/department/area" was just a smidgen behind the previous traits in importance. Of lesser importance, but mentioned by 51% of our top executives, was *"being visible* or networking well." And 45% said "being tenacious," or "having a stick-to-it-until-the-job-is-done attitude," was also an essential trait.

Our executives are reacting to changing times and facing globally competitive markets. They need to put more focus on being productive and efficient. The technology age seems to have pushed top management to focus on achieving goals faster and reacting to changes more quickly, so as not to get left behind.

Ten years ago, "politically aligned" was a trait high on many executives' lists of desired characteristics—today, only 8% selected "politically aligned" as a needed skill to earn a promotion, while 92% said it was not influential at all.

I often hear clients complain, "Why is it some people seem to be so lucky? You know, the ones who land the plum projects, biggest raises, and fast-track promotions." People envy colleagues who get promoted for being smarter, luckier, cleverer, prettier, or a great schmoozer. Some just write them off as workaholics and say devoting every waking hour to a career is not how they want to live their lives.

"None of those traits make someone a star at work," said management consultant Robert Kelley, Carnegie Mellon professor and author of *How to Be a Star at Work* (Times, 1999).

"It's actually how they do their job and some specific strategies that allow these 'stars' to outshine other employees. We ran

employees through our training program and, according to their
bosses, their productivity shot up 40% on average."

You have within you all the qualities necessary for success. No
one will excel to great heights unless two factors are in place.
You must love your work and possess the skills to do your job,
Kelley noted. You must also have the desire to spend time and
energy on improving the company's bottom line.

Kelley reported many commonly held productivity enhanc-
ers, such as clean desks, computer programs, and time management sequencers, clearly don't influence a person's productivity.
But learning star traits do. Kelley's thirteen years of research
identified nine work strategies and pointed out that women
specifically struggle with initiative, networking, and teamwork.

"Forget offering to plan the office Christmas party or simple
ways to do your job better. Stars go above and beyond their
job description and focus on offering new ideas that result in
bottom-line increases and volunteer to follow the initiatives
through to completion," he said. Kelley stresses that the star's
initiative almost always helps out people other than himself—
typically other employees or the department.

Networking has taken on a new and global twist. As we become more of a knowledge-based society, finding the correct or
needed information becomes a necessity. "Work stars develop a
network—often using email—to reach experts and get the information they need. The goal is to develop relationships that
allow you to obtain needed knowledge in the best and quickest
way possible. But networking is a two-way street. You must also
establish yourself as a resource and share your knowledge with
those who need it," he pointed out.

Teamwork is a prized attribute, but not all team activities are
productive or lead to promotions. Kelley revealed some accurate
insights, cautioning people when they are recruited to be on
various teams. "Don't be a flatterer," he warned. "Team commitments can become productivity traps, draining time and energy
from the critical company path and chewing up many hours

from work and leisure time. When asked to be on a team, you should evaluate what your value will be and how it'll affect your career advancement. Most teams' results rarely make much difference, and months later few remember who was on the team." Teams can often spread you too thin, conveying a message that you don't manage commitments well, added Kelley. He suggested you be choosy and wisely select only those commitments that are being closely watched by upper management.

Kelley's research concluded that you must also train yourself to look at your job, your department, and your company as a whole, from a global perspective—what matters to bosses and top management in achieving the organization's missions or goals. That seems to be the key to finding productivity solutions and becoming invaluable.

Additionally, we find there are also a few other specific skills needed to advance. In today's world, computer skills are essential and necessary—for many jobs you simply must possess them. Many executives mentioned that listening skills have become a lost art, but they're a necessity for a manager or executive.

Communication skills, both verbal and written, were repeatedly noted as important and impressive. You won't sail to the top if you can't express your ideas clearly and easily. Take courses, practice, or work with a mentor until you have mastered communicating with all levels of staff and management. Pay extra attention to your emails. People send quick responses, full of typos, skipped words, and misspellings—others notice these errors and miss the content of the message. Spend the extra minute to use the spell checker and proofread your communications.

Team building is an essential skill for advancing to senior and top management positions. Jim Medzegian, who has served in top management at the Boeing Company and who also sits on the board of trustees for a large college, has seen teams in action in community, governmental, and corporate environments. He explains why team building is a prized trait to many top executives. "No *one* of us is as smart as *all* of us (collectively). Teams working toward a common goal, with a common process, provide an *exponential* increase in capacity, creativity, and results." It's the team, not a single individual, that achieves results. The individual fosters the results.

An executive at one of the country's top ten largest companies shared his insight. "You cannot rise to the top of an organization that's large like ours unless you are able to team build," said this executive, whose company has nearly two hundred thousand employees. "Most people on the rise realize that they can't produce results alone. Indeed, you, as a manager, must shape your team, set goals, motivate, manage, and train your team members! You need to get the most productivity from each member. You must foster a can-do attitude and ask for input and continuous improvements. Building your team to contribute results is the goal. It is these results that influence top or upper management decision makers to promote you. I've seen some 'stars' who excelled in team building. They also networked well, serving on key committees upper management cared about. These people got promotion, after promotion, after promotion—and their rise was quick and fast," he reported.

The workplace of today and tomorrow requires high-level skills in technology, communications, and interaction with others, plus budgeting and assessement of corporate goals. These are the essential basics that produce results. As you move up, you need to develop and master these skills.

Computer skills are vital, so improve your proficiency with the programs that you use in your office. You might want to expand and then learn a new application that you could use if you moved up to a different position or even to a new organization.

What are the other skills employers say they want? *Initiative!* Many times it's your own suggested improvements that will make a project come off in a better light or that will improve a system or a process that you have been doing in your department. Be open to new ideas. Go to your boss when you have an idea. Offer many. Management might not run with every one you put forth, but you will be seen as someone who shows initiative. Always be looking at ways to be able to do things faster, more efficiently, more accurately, in a more timely manner.

A president of a $125 million company noted that most people's biggest career mistake is that they fail to promote their value to their own organization. Volunteer to head a project. Offer to organize a committee or plan an event. Suggest that you'd be willing to research some potential equipment purchases and write up your recommendations. Volunteer to be the one to try out a new computer system. Assist in hiring a new staff person. Train him or her. Use your initiative and efforts to expand your duties and skills and learn more on the job. Focus on improvements, and before you know it, your supervisor and your manager's supervisor will be noticing you.

Diversifying your abilities will enhance your marketability. There are people you'll encounter who will try to pigeonhole you into one slot. You might experience the "Oh, you're a nurse, what could you possibly know about marketing?" attitude. You need to actively broaden your knowledge base. Join organizations and read trade journals and books to enlarge your knowledge and expertise, not narrow it. Employers want adaptable workers—flexible enough to learn new things. Share your ideas and *be innovative*. Be a *global thinker*—not just about your career, but about the company as a whole.

Employers value managerial skills, though today people are judged by results more often than just the ability to get along or supervise well. Today's managers act more like coaches and less like the dictatorial bosses of years past. The coaches set out game plans and allow individuals to take responsibility for how they're going to get the job done. They make team members accountable and foster the individual autonomy that is vital to achieving company goals and future success. *Today's leaders are people who get results—from themselves, their teams, and their areas.*

Many top CEOs and presidents have reported that the one skill they want managers to have is an understanding of how the financial operations of the organization work. Don't confuse this with just managing a budget. You must have bottom-line responsibility, experience, and a key understanding of profits and losses.

Budgets require planning skills and a resourceful use of funds. But rising stars go further and acquire knowledge of the company's overall financial operations. David Lightfoot, a former CEO and company president, is now a CFO at a $150 million development company. He offered these insights. "Understanding the organization's financial picture is essential. I've never seen a manager get by without having a grasp of it. It's hard to produce results unless you can understand the big picture. Ultimately, cash, then people, are the lifeblood of any organization. Without cash to pay the bills, there will be no people, because your organization will cease to exist."

Financial operations are the bottom line, whether it's a nonprofit or a corporation—everything comes down to dollars and cents. Whether you are a "numbers" person or not, you must be able to work with, manage, and be resourceful with the money you handle and oversee. Doing more with less, cutting or containing costs, and producing bottom-line impacts while you achieve results always gets noticed. Learn about financial operations management. Sit down with someone in the accounting office and learn about cash flow, profit, loss, and the overall financial picture. You might consider volunteering for a nonprofit or charity group as the treasurer or a board member to learn exactly how decisions are based on both potential outcomes and costs.

In conclusion, many senior executives said most employees don't have a big-picture perspective. They look at their little domain as the whole universe, instead of seeing themselves as a spoke in the wheel. You need to "think globally," so many said. This means understanding and responding to the organization's goals, objectives, and financial operations. Everyone needs to understand what it is the company is selling, be it a service, a product, or a mission objective. You need to think globally and strategically about better ways to improve yourself, your area, and your company. You must make suggestions and changes that clearly address and advance the organization's goals and objectives, thus contributing to the success of the overall operation.

Several CEOS said they look for people who add value to the company, process, or team and deem them an "asset." Focus on adding value by continually examining how you are taking charge of your job and showing initiative to do it better. You must be flexible. *A competitive advantage you can develop is to become flexible and adaptable to meet your employer's changing needs.* Be willing to try new things that haven't been done before. The rate of change in the workplace is incredibly fast and growing exponentially. Many people feel insecure and resist change, but employers continue to seek out and promote those who've demonstrated that they are flexible and adapt easily to change.

Our top executives all lead by example. Do as they do and *develop a strong work ethic.* Many mentioned this as a necessary and admired trait. There are two ways to approach your work—the first is with a nine-to-five mentality that it's a job and a paycheck. The second approach is the "my career is a career with a future" framework. When you do only what's required—never volunteering, never adding more—the results are usually stagnation in professional development. Top corporate executives continuously tell me they need "value added" employees—those who bring more to their jobs. The mind-set "I can't do it" never accomplishes anything, but "I will try" performs wonders.

Being recognized as a good, productive worker—dependable, with initiative to improve and the ability to bring quality to your job—will make you more visible to the upper echelon in your organization.

Network . . . Network . . . Network

Of our top executives surveyed, 90% said networking was important to their career rise and remained important to them.

Developing a lifelong list of contacts and professional associates will help your career immensely. Whether you're trying to solve a work problem, looking for a new job, just trying to get new ideas in your field or area, being involved in a professional association can help you manage your career. You also can't expect to network only when you need a job.

Our top executives noted that serving on their committees is the top way to network with them. Over two-thirds identified this as a key strategy. But if you're looking to move up, it's critical to carefully select the appropriate committees—many recommend just volunteering to serve if you aren't asked. Several executives said that being active in professional associations was a terrific way to network and develop your career. This has to be an ongoing process, however, not just something you do on your job search days. The benefits of serving on committees are learning new skills and meeting contacts—both great ways to advance your career.

Tracy Brown, deputy executive director for the Washington Society of CPAs pointed out, "Volunteering for committees and being involved in special events allows many people to meet and know you. These are terrific places if your company is small or large, because you meet others who are often instrumental in helping you move on to bigger and better positions after they get to know you. Sooner or later, almost everyone does a job search, so all committee contacts can be sources of leads. Sometimes they call to recruit you to apply at their company when they have an opening. Working with other key industry leaders in various association activities is a great way to be seen, get noticed, and obtain career or job advice. It's really an essential career management strategy everyone should utilize and develop," she said. "I've seen firsthand where a member in our association took on a committee role or task—for example, chaired a conference—and then other members saw the outcome he or she produced, realized that this was a talented person, and then approached and offered the volunteer a great job."

This top executive's point is well taken. Everyone knows the club's president or the conference's coordinator. Volunteering allows you to become, and remain, known. Also, associations are excellent places to develop new skills or hone current ones.

Another key strategy our top executives cited for networking and getting to know them was through working a charity event—for example, fund-raising alumni events, such as college capital campaigns, benefit galas, and auctions. Community activities, such as local politics or community events or festivals, are also good ways to meet and get to know key leaders. These are outside activities that anyone can get involved with.

The next popular suggestion was to actually volunteer to work on the CEO's or top executive's pet project. You'll sure get to meet them that way. Also, calling up executives and asking them directly for a brief meeting, coffee, or lunch to meet and network was recommended. In fact, the direct approach was much more popular than playing golf or attending other sports and recreational events specifically as effective networking opportunities. Our top executives liked a direct approach, particularly the college presidents, hospital administrators, and nonprofit directors.

Although *Golf* magazine has labeled golf the premier networking activity of the next decade, our group of CEOs and top executives said it's absolutely not. Less than 5% named golf as a way to network with them. The few who did were women— only one man mentioned golf, and he's a business owner who

Effective ways to network with top executives, in order of their preferences:

1. Serve on committees with them.
2. Work on charitable or community activities with them.
3. Volunteer for their pet projects.
4. Get to know them through social engagements.

said he loved the sport and would play it with anybody. (Note: Many salespeople, though, find playing golf with clients and potential customers an excellent way to get and keep business.)

A few other networking tips to remember:

- **Be active in a professional association.** Being chairman of a committee is an excellent way to increase your visibility. Others will see you and get to know you. This is a great way to be the first person people think of when recruiting a new employee or manager to work for their organization. Many, many association leadership positions or roles have led to great new jobs for those who have been actively involved over a long period of time. Build your network wisely. Offer help to those who seek you out, and develop new friendships with people whose careers you admire—people with authoritative positions you'd like someday to hold.

- **Network internally.** If you are currently at a large organization, there are thousands of people inside your company. You can make many contacts who will help you perform better on the job and alert you to new opportunities in different divisions if you develop a network that consists of others in various departments and areas.

- **Become a resource for others.** You'll become known and others will think of you not only when they need help, but also when a good job opens up. If you help others, they'll be more likely to pass job leads your way or even try to recruit you for positions at their company.

- **Set goals for making network connections.** Time pressures require us to choose wisely the groups we join or meetings we attend. Always have a list of five or six key people in the group whom you'd like to meet, and look for opportunities to introduce yourself and work on projects or committees they're on.

- **When attending conferences, trade shows, or major meetings, decide in advance what you hope to learn, and try to meet two or three people you can spend time with and call again in the future.** "Working the room" to take home two dozen cards from people who are clueless as to who you are will be of little or no help later. Introduce yourself using a memory tag, such as "I'm Shannon Bender, a loan officer for Chase Manhattan Bank." Memory tags help people better remember who you are and what you do. If you are unemployed, simply say, "Hello, I'm Tom Maxwell, a project manager." If they ask whom you work for, state, "I left recently and am currently looking for a new position." Don't be embarrassed or afraid to mention this—they may know of a potential job. Often, when I teach my seminars I ask the crowd, "How many of you enjoy meeting strangers?" Less than 10% raise their hands. Unfortunately, you must take the initiative when you attend conferences. Approach a few people you wish to meet and contact them again when the conference is over to nurture the new relationship. Email is great for this.

Other networking tips you'll find helpful include the following:
- Call people up and simply ask their advice.
- Suggest lunch.
- Develop relationships by calling, sending notes or emails, and passing on articles or resources of interest.
- Use thank-you notes liberally, showing gratitude whenever warranted.
- Applaud the success of others—everyone likes to be recognized. Send a card or short note of congratulations following a promotion, new job, or other important achievement.
- Make time for your network. Return phone calls or emails within twenty-four hours. Someone with a pressing business problem needs your help now, not in a week or two. You can

always limit a call by saying, "I have a meeting in ten minutes," but you'll create more friends (as well as appear professional) when you return calls promptly.

Ask for what you need. Never assume someone won't help
you—*ask*. Our CEOs, time after time, said, "If you want something specific from me, call and ask for it."

One client, Kathleen, got a big promotion because she volunteered and worked on the planning committee representing her
department when the company was looking at a major companywide computer systems upgrade. She met several people in
other departments, and since her company was quite large, she'd
never had any interaction with these various departments.
When she wanted to move up, she began to network, inviting
different people to lunch. One day, a committee person told her
about a new program their division was going to add, saying her
boss's manager just mentioned they'd be needing to get some
leadership and a director. The contact agreed to pass on Kathleen's resumé to her boss's boss—and from this came an interview and a new promotion for Kathleen, with a big, healthy
raise.

This kind of networking happens inside companies every day.
Of course, networking is also a key success factor when looking
for new jobs with other organizations. According to the Department of Labor, 63% of all new jobs were found through contacts
in the last year. Networking can be a key component when it's
time to job hunt, so maintain a good network by being actively
involved on a continual basis.

To summarize, it appears our top executives are advising you
to network, to make career choices that will allow you to take on
leadership roles, improve your department, and add to the overall
system. Always look for ways to save money or improve a process,
system, or project—later, you'll have noted results from your efforts to report to future employers. Remember, it's those initiatives—the little bit extra you do, the personal excellence you

bring to your job, and the activities you take on—that allow you to develop a great resumé. Once you start living this success orientation philosophy, terrific opportunities will come your way.

CEOs Reveal What It Takes to Get to the Top

Top executives think differently, act differently, and are incredibly passionate about what they do. There are some key lessons to be learned from them. I've quoted and summarized both my survey results and the information I've gleaned from personal conversations. You'll want to emulate some of the traits, behaviors, attitudes, and strategies they mentioned. These people know what success is—they live it every day. Their insights will help you gain tools you can use to succeed at any job, in any field, especially if the goal you set for yourself is to reach the top.

The results were quite conclusive. Those who head organizations attribute their success to hard work, being a good problem solver, and being an honest person with integrity who knows how to focus on priorities.

There seems to be unilateral agreement among top executives that hard work is a required ingredient for getting ahead and succeeding. Hard work also requires time. A great deal of it must be invested in your career if your goal is to continue to move up.

"Hard work" translates on average into sixty-two hours per week for our top executives. No one who responded to the survey put in less than forty-five hours per week. About 10% admitted they worked one hundred or more hours per week. Most said they reported scheduled hours but did not count commuting, emails, other work done at home, or required evening or weekend events or meetings. My best guess is that those activities would add another ten to fifteen hours or more to their work weeks.

On top of this, 80% of our top executives travel for their jobs. The average number of nights that our surveyed executives spent away from home was forty-eight per year. One CEO noted, "I chose this company because of my family, so that I would not be on the road more than ten days a year."

Several top executives mentioned they had learned to work smarter, not longer, though one CEO, whose organization makes hundreds of millions, noted, "Never equate long hours with working smarter. If you really want to get ahead, work smarter and work longer hours—that's been a winning combination for me and others I've seen."

Conceded—people at the top and those striving to get there work hard to do it. I've pointed this out so you can clearly see the sacrifices it takes to move to the president's slot or run your own company. Some people who read this might acknowledge this fact and decide to go a different road. They might simply find a job they enjoy working at—either part-time or full-time, but with no extra time involved beyond that. Still others accept the long hours and hard work as part of the process, admitting it "comes with the territory to rise to the top." The challenges, rewards, and excitement of the job make it all worth it. You need to decide what works for you.

Increase Your Competitive Advantage with These Tools

This section will give you specific tools you can use to move ahead, land a promotion, and plot out your career.

The price of success is much lower than the price of failure.

Productivity Monitor

Since top executives say it's critical to produce results, it's important to document your skills and on-the-job accomplishments. This chart, called the Productivity Monitor, is the basic makeup of future resumés—so keep the skills and accomplishments detailed with size, numbers, percentages, increases, or decreases. Do note any cost or time savings.

The technique is to keep a brief monthly record of work accomplishments and activities that substantiate your on-the-job contributions. *The purpose* is to track your career accomplishments. *Your record of on-the-job productivity influences raises and promotions.*

Specifically, your record has these uses:

- During performance reviews, you can duplicate your list and give it to your boss. It's quite effective to "remind" bosses of "forgotten" contributions.
- It shows "proof" or evidence of your performance and productivity to "justify" a raise or salary increase.
- It can be used to show job growth and adaptability in handling new duties as you seek an internal promotion.
- It documents accomplishments as they are completed, noting important contributions to be added to your resumé. Statistics, numbers, percentages, and savings should all be noted.

For example, Jane was a regional sales manager for a large pharmaceutical company. One-third of her bonus was tied to "outreach and new marketing activities." Her Productivity Monitor was an important record of the numerous skills she brought to her company. Over time, her Productivity Monitor has helped her get raises, even in years when most other senior managers didn't. And it has assisted in landing her several promotions. Each month she notes accomplishments—sales, hiring new staff, trade show results, and the like.

Then, on December 31, she summarizes her major resumé accomplishments for the year: Sold eleven units (her quota was eight—that's 140% over quota). Moved her region to #2 in sales revenues, up from #8 (fourteen total regions). Received a corporate "Outstanding Manager of the Year" award. Implemented a computer system for online sales reports and saved reps five hours per week, reducing costs by 22%. The information from her annual Productivity Monitor is used to inform her boss of her accomplishments and later enhance her resumé for the day she decides to move on.

This is an important career management tool to record your activities. You can simply highlight the major points, as Jane did, or you can be more detailed on daily/weekly activities. Create your tracking device to aid you in substantiating and "reminding" your organization just how valuable and indispensable you are.

A major advantage of the Productivity Monitor is that you actually write down significant contributions to be noted on your resumé. It's a wise practice to update your resumé at least once a year. Don't let good opportunities pass you by because you lack a current resumé. (For more help on resumés, consult my book *Winning Resumés,* published by John Wiley & Sons and available through my website, www.robinryan.com.)

Performance Chart

Jobs change. The longer you stay in an organization performing a specific job, the more change and adaptation the job is likely to go through. Duties assigned when you got hired five years ago might be very different from those you perform in the same position today. If you seek a promotion or a raise, you'll find the performance chart a good tool to use.

The technique is to compare responsibility changes from your original job description to your current job duties, as well as note significant accomplishments. *Most likely your job has increased in responsibility. Note the additions when asking for a raise or promotion.*

The purpose is to draw attention to the additional responsibilities and level of growth you've achieved on the job to support a request for your employer to realign your job to the actual (and higher) level of current responsibilities and performance. When asking for a promotion, you can easily show the major difference between what you were originally hired to do and all the new duties you now perform. This chart clearly shows the "extras" often taken for granted by bosses simply because you've added and done them over time. This chart also provides evidence when asking for a raise that bases the request on the fact that additional (or more advanced) responsibilities have been assigned but neither salary nor title has been increased or changed to compensate for these additional contributions.

Stephanie Slattery worked in office administration for a large telephone company. Highly productive, she possessed many talents that she applied to her job. She'd been there almost two and a half years when a new boss took over her department. Within a few months, the new boss called Stephanie into his office and praised her for all she was doing in her job. He noticed she did a great deal more than her job description required. He suggested she write a letter noting her original duties and then include all her current activities. He'd support her, but she'd have to do all the work herself and go through the union and proper personnel channels. Stephanie picked up the ball and created this chart to more clearly demonstrate she was now performing a "higher level" job. She was thorough in the hopes of persuading her company to give her a promotion. It worked—she obtained a *5 grade promotion* and a *$15,000 raise!*

Note: Some jobs don't have formal job descriptions. In that case, create one, noting original duties assigned, as best you remember, and exactly what you are doing now.

PERFORMANCE CHART—STEPHANIE SLATTERY		
Old	**New**	**Contributions**
Served as office clerk within department.	Maintains the computerized tracking systems for department. Handles all computer systems troubleshooting.	Worked as department liaison with IT to install an entire new computer network system into department.
Provided the maintenance, compilation, preparation, and certification of claim records and reports.	Trains other staff on all computer systems, updates computer training manuals.	Trained staff managers on new system usage.
Typed records and reports.	Coordinates software and systems modifications. Interacts with IT for corporate networking integrations.	Coordinated all software usage and enhancements on system.
Talked with customers to obtain claim information.	Created and coordinates all invoicing and computerized billing invoicing systems with sophisticated tracking mechanisms.	Developed customized reports, budgeting spreadsheets, invoice and claims tracking systems.
Prepared and verified claims bills.	Generates reports.	Provided more data and statistics for executive assistance to the Division Manager.
Typed letters to customers on claim notification.	Provides secretarial support exclusively to the Division Manager,	

Old	New	Contributions
	including calendar scheduling, travel arrangements, meeting coordination, and mail sorting.	
Filed.	Provides project management.	
Needed skills: typing, adding machine, copying, fax.		

Moving into Management

A top executive at a Fortune 100 company offered a candid view of the over one hundred thousand employees who worked for the organization. He said, "Many people say they want to be in management, but few earn the right." He noted that today's workplace requires leaders who possess the experience and behavioral traits needed to continue the company's success. He cited the need to "be able to get along with people" and the ability "to get things done in a team." You as an individual must add value to the whole.

This executive (whose career to the top is one most people would envy) prescribed the ideal for the manager he wants to hire or promote to meet today's and tomorrow's business challenges. He said, "The new manager must be an excellent performer with high ethical standards. The person must be committed to the company's principles, goals, and standards. Producing results must be an important priority. The manager must treat people with respect and trust and earn the same for himself or herself from those he/she works with. He/she must promote teamwork and empower others. The person needs to demonstrate innovation and seek intellectual growth and learning. You must share information, be an open communicator, and, above all, listen." This is the new criteria by which his company judges employees for management and advancement roles.

Do you have what it takes to be a manager?

Self-Assessment: Evaluate Your Ability to Become a Good Manager

- **Have you gotten more training?** Getting additional education is the fastest way to move ahead. Debra Lorie, a hospital medical records specialist, dreamed of being a manager. She went to college at night and sacrificed six years of hard work to get her bachelor's degree. She took out student loans and financed the rest from her paycheck. When she combined her work experience and new diploma, she landed a healthcare manager position at Pacific Medical with a salary increase of $7,000 per year and had three promotions in the two years that followed. Thomas, a full-time worker at a local bank, went to graduate school for four years to earn his MBA. It was a continuous challenge and sacrifice giving up almost all his other life as he held a job while he took the courses. After he graduated, he began an aggressive job search that landed him a terrific marketing position as a manager for an emerging technology company. Two years later he was making twice the salary he'd left. Obtaining a degree is not always necessary to move ahead, but getting essential skills to do the job is. More training is likely needed for you to move ahead.

- **Have you coached others effectively?** Psychotherapist Daneen Skube, a *Seattle Times* columnist who advises people on interpersonal communications in the workplace, noted, "People who clearly do not have the capacity for learning the technical skills required for a job may be promoted once but don't continue up the chain of command once their incapacity is discovered. However, people who are liked by others, who possess the emotional intelligence to get along at work, often make excellent managers. They know how to resolve conflicts between employees; listen to ideas and find middle ground; persuade others to help them and their team; and negotiate in stressful situations. Organizations are always on the lookout for employees who already have these people skills. If you really want to make yourself more competitive and you know you're already highly technically competent, don't just continue to get more technical skills. Look into training opportunities, coaching, or books that will enhance your interpersonal skills," she recommended. Ask yourself: Do I give clear directions? Do I look to solve problems instead of assigning blame? Do I check to see that the work is progressing correctly and in a timely fashion? Do I recognize that there are multiple ways to get a job done well? Do I easily encourage people? These are important abilities necessary to success. To gain experience, you can offer to train newly hired people on computer and other office procedures or offer to oversee temporary workers. You can volunteer to head up a committee or project or join an association and take on a leadership role there.

- **Are you a decision maker?** Managers can't sit on the fence forever. They need to evaluate problems, look at or ask for solutions, and then decide. You can't get held up by the fact that you can and will make mistakes. Deciding is key. One national franchise owner said, "I promote the 'find-a-way make-a-way' person, since I know this is someone I can trust to get the job done." Achievers make decisions and in the end are right much more often than they are wrong.

- **Can you delegate?** Delegating is a necessary skill, since managers must assign work, plan projects, and make numerous

choices daily. Delegating goes hand in hand with releasing
control and giving employees autonomy in their jobs rather
than micromanaging them. You won't get far without mastering this skill.

- **Are you a resourceful problem solver?** As a manager you
must make decisions, be resourceful, and find solutions to
problems. Hone these skills, since "good decision making and
problem solving" are key skills our surveyed top executives
notice. Deputy Executive Director Tracy Brown stated,
"When coming to me with a problem, bring a solution with
you. It doesn't have to be the right solution, but it shows you
are at least trying to solve the problem and not add to it."
Many of our executives echoed this desire.

- **Do you take on more responsibility while demonstrating initiative and productivity?** Do you make a habit of asking for
more work and expanding the scope of your current job? Do
you contribute new ideas to improve your department or office? Can you adjust easily to change?

  Jeanne MacGregor, an executive secretary for Brown and
Cole, a large manufacturer, volunteered for a big project,
planning a major company conference. She used this opportunity to really show what she could do. Jeanne surpassed her
boss's expectations in planning and pulling off a highly successful event. She efficiently organized and procured food,
lodging, and speakers, saving her company a significant
amount of money. Top executives took notice, and within
three months she was promoted into management.

- **How strong are your communication skills?** Learn to listen,
explain clearly, and give understandable directions. Today's
communication skills also mean using technology—computers, Internet, voice mail, teleconferencing—to transmit information. Both oral and written skills are paramount to your

management success. Practice speaking and facilitating meetings. Volunteer to serve on office committees, and be an active participant. You can improve your written skills by writing more reports, articles for newsletters, composing correspondence, or taking classes.

- **Are you a good listener?** Employees like managers who ask for and listen to their ideas and suggestions. They feel more understood when you listen attentively to their requests or needs or while they outline a problem. Practice learning to let a person explain while you nod and take in what's being said. Do not interrupt. Managers need to allow others to express themselves completely, no matter how hurried or pressured you may be. You need to hear everything, then formulate your response after you've interpreted what has been said. You'll be called on to resolve conflicts, smooth over problems, and encourage your team to work together. Listen first, then decide.

- **Have you observed and emulated good managers?** Moving into management requires different attitudes, perspectives, interpersonal skills, and a professional presentation. Study managers you respect. How assertive are they? What abilities identify them as good managers? How do they think and make decisions? Emulate their strengths to develop your own skills. Whenever possible, find a mentor. Learn how to handle problems by watching how your mentor resolves tricky issues. Ask for his or her recommendations on books on how to motivate others and manage workloads.

  People always work hardest and are most loyal to managers who praise and reward their good work. Develop that pattern.

- **Do you operate with high professional standards and ethics?** Our top executives said this was of particularly high concern to them. Upper management seeks out managers who display integrity and honesty. Ask yourself: Do I respect other employees? Do I treat everyone as equals and harbor no prejudices against minorities, foreigners, the disabled, or homosexuals? Am I careful not to use terminology that others might deem offensive? Do I treat all people fairly? In today's workplace, you must show a high level of integrity and demonstrate no actions or words that could be seen as sexual harassment or discriminatory. You must evaluate people by their skill and merit, nothing else.

- **Do you have the self-confidence to assert yourself?** To become a manager, you must take action and plan. Work hard to improve professionally. Your self-concept must allow you to envision yourself as a manager and act like one long before you're likely to move ahead.

  Debra, our medical records specialist, found that her coworkers at the hospital disagreed with her efforts to gain more schooling. They didn't cheer her on; instead they told her she was wasting her time and working too hard. Debra realized the truth—if she became a manager, she'd no longer be like them. Once she stopped listening to all the "naysayers," it became easier to achieve success. She didn't let others dissuade her with comments like "You work too hard" or "Why do you bother?" Jeanne, our executive secretary, knew she could plan out a successful event. She used lunch hours and some time at home to determine what had been done before, to learn what the group's preferences were. She negotiated the catering and accommodations with a tone of authority. She not only saved money but added to the creativity that made the event memorable for everyone there—particularly upper management. Both women's extra efforts moved their careers along.

- **Can you handle pressure deadlines, set and meet goals, and achieve results?** The higher you go, the more stress and pressure you'll likely encounter. You need to develop coping mechanisms that let you handle the challenge but not burn out. You need to acquire good time management and planning skills. As your workload (and the number of people under you) increases, you need to become well organized to ensure you make company goals. Having to put out small fires gives you the foundation to deal more effectively with the bigger problems as they arise. When uncertain, smart managers ask their bosses or colleagues for advice, ideas, and guidance.

Different Avenues for the Move up to Management

Most people will receive a promotion at their current company. They might move up into their boss's job when the boss vacates the position. They might move up to fill another management vacancy. Or they could get the chance to be a supervisor when a brand-new position is created.

Judy was a community college instructor. After the college went through some big changes, a few new jobs opened up and a new position, administrator of instruction, was created. That was the job Judy was promoted into. She had only teaching experience prior to this promotion, but she had learned several other key management skills through volunteering for and working on various committees.

Stephen made his move into management in a more unique way—one that's effective and happens often. I went into a Waldenbooks store to make a purchase, and Stephen cashed me out. His name tag read "Store Manager." When I handed him my credit card, he glanced at the name and said, "Robin Ryan— it's you. You wrote the book *60 Seconds & You're Hired!*" I smiled and said, "Yes." He continued, "I heard your seminar at Barnes & Noble when I was a retail clerk there, praying I would someday run my own bookstore. It was all I ever dreamed about, but it seemed like no one noticed all my hard effort. You talked about interviewing and promotions and said sometimes the only way to move up is to leave and move on. That got me thinking. I worked hard, put an action plan in place, and landed this job as the store manager. I'd still be waiting for Barnes & Noble to notice me if I'd stayed. Now I'm in line for a bigger store and eventually a corporate job," he reported.

The moral of these stories: Where there's a will, there's a way. If your company is failing to notice you, many times the answer is to do as Stephen did—move on. You can often fulfill your dream and land a management job, particularly when you leave a large employer and move to a smaller company. Likewise, employees of small businesses, in which the owner runs the company, often *must* move on to fulfill management dreams, as the owner already has and will most likely keep the job you want.

When the Best Way to Get Ahead Is to *Move On*

Fact: *The biggest raises almost always come by quitting your job and moving on to a new employer.* These often are moves up, too, all at the same time.

You may do everything possible in your current organization, and still a promotion may elude you. Less qualified people may move up. Less competent or docile people may be the ones who got promoted. Those less driven, less innovative, may get the promotion you are hoping for and want. Sometimes promotions don't seem fair. When this happens, as it may, you need to make appropriate career choices that are right for you.

Opportunities in large organizations, where promotions used to be very common and regular, are disappearing fast. In the past, most promotions involved jobs breaking into, as well as those moving up, the middle-management ranks. These are the very jobs that have been downsized and totally eliminated. Today and in the future, more people will find themselves in organizations where there is nowhere to go.

Tina was a program manager and had a good job with a large scientific organization that had twenty-five thousand employees. She told me that since it was a very male-dominated field, she had been unable to get a promotion. We discussed the facts, and I encouraged Tina to investigate other departments in her organization. Two months later she saw a new job—in the training and program development area. She applied, sailed through the interview, and easily persuaded them to offer her the job. Tina was pleased, told her current boss, and moved to her new position in the new department. It was definitely a promotion and an interesting job. The most influential factor in the end was that it was a promotion and it paid $5,000 more. As a single parent, she felt the additional money would provide many extras and allow her to qualify for a remodeling loan to update her modest house. She did very well in the position. Thirteen months after she'd moved on, a new division head position was created in her old department. She was recruited back with a new promotion and another salary increase. Sometimes you may need to look beyond your immediate area, as Tina did. My clients have moved to other departments inside their company and seen their careers bloom. Whether it's more interesting, a different manager, or new eyes observing and listening to you, a new area can take your career out of neutral.

For many people, the best way to move ahead will be to move on to a completely new and different employer. According to the Small Business Administration, two out of every three new jobs created in America in the last year were with small employers (fewer than one hundred employees). In tiny organizations, often the only place to go is somewhere else. For example, Tim was an accountant for a small company. As the company grew into a multimillion-dollar-per-year entity, his duties increased.

So did the hours. He averaged between seventy and eighty hours a week and could not get the owners to give him a staff person or much of a raise. He wanted the title of controller, which was the job he was doing. The owner, fearful that he'd want too much money, kept refusing. Tim looked at his options. Moving on seemed the only solution. We worked on his resumé, and indeed he quickly got hired as an assistant controller, with better benefits and an $11,000 salary boost. Just recently, his new company promoted him to the controller position.

Decisions on promotions—getting one or not getting one—will likely be the most influential factors in your career decisions. Always seek advice from respected colleagues and senior managers. A qualified career counselor can offer objective insight and might be a worthwhile investment of time and money to help gain a clear perspective. But in the end, the career you create is your own. If you don't like your situation or what you are doing—change it.

Making the Most of Your Current Job

If you feel stymied in your progress, take a long, thorough look at what you want. One client, Mark, a state budget analyst, said, "I got so frustrated at my department and bosses when I couldn't get promoted. I was shocked when a higher-level manager took me aside one day and said, 'Unless you change your behavior and attitude, you'll go no farther.' It was demoralizing but also eye-opening. I got frightened and defensive, but I did think it over. He gave me so many examples—'You never work extra, or try to improve anything, you don't demonstrate leadership, never volunteer for projects or committees, you're negative and express strong opinions that distress other employees.' The person told me in a coaching, helpful way, but I still felt devastated. I guess I just felt I deserved the promotion because I'd been there so long."

"Entitlement" is the syndrome, and many people have it. They justify their wants by "I deserve it." Many managers and top executives identified this as a serious problem they face.

Career progression is a series of choices, behaviors, performances, and opportunities. Mark's examination of his behavior and attitude was the first part of his professional changes. His first response? He got angry, mailed out resumés—even got a job offer with another state agency. It was a good opportunity—a challenging position setting up a new division. But he was also realistic and knew it would require long hours for an indefinite period of time. When we discussed the offer together, he was hesitant. I told Mark, "Career choices are just that—choices. You create your life. You must decide, based on your values and what you honestly want for yourself." He had three small children at home, and the long hours would keep him away a great deal. How "hard" you wish to work is a choice only you can make. But I've not seen too many people who rose through the ranks working only forty hours a week. As you get past the first management levels, the jobs are stressful, and often the higher you go the more pressure you are under.

So Mark, our budget analyst—although he was frustrated about not being promoted—chose not to move on to the new job. He did follow my advice and began to behave differently at the job he had. After a couple of coaching sessions, he put new energy into his current job and adopted a better attitude toward work. He volunteered to be on a committee. Since he enjoyed using computers, he worked with a couple of staff people to teach them some more sophisticated computer application processes. He made himself into a kind of internal technical support resource. Mark had truly changed. Eventually his managers acknowledged that it wasn't a short-term, but a permanent improvement.

Fourteen months after our first meeting, Mark got a promotion. He wrote to say: "When I changed, the job seemed to get better. I have been given a great deal more computer systems to oversee. I really enjoy it. It's so easy for me. I never thought I'd ever be happy here, but I admit, now I am."

Mark learned some valuable lessons about achieving career satisfaction. He realized you can define your own work tasks. By using your natural talents (often viewed by yourself as "easy work"), you can ask for and develop the more interesting parts of your job. Also, a positive, cooperative attitude increases your ability to work and get things done as a team (required management skills). In fact, the grass may be pretty green in your current job if you apply yourself and challenge yourself to find areas for improvement. Remember, you can volunteer to take on new duties and/or get duties reassigned to try out new skills or work in capacities you find more enjoyable.

When you care about your job, it shows. You have more pride, you produce higher-quality results. Your attitude and willingness to adapt and change through extra effort can produce the biggest change of all—turning your current job into one much more to your liking.

Summary

Don't let anybody else tell you what you should or shouldn't do. Set your own goals. Don't try to live through the dreams of your parents or your spouse or your friends. Only you know exactly what makes you happy. You change, your interests change, and, sadly, life happens, so when you're defining your career goals, you need to reevaluate them often—no less than once a year, reevaluate where you are going and what you want. Be productive when you manage your career. Keep track of your results and be sure that upper management is aware of them, too. The workplace keeps changing—so stay tuned to new and different trends. There may be a new skill you'd like to pick up. Do it! Keep on learning. Perhaps you would like to try something different at the office. Go to your boss and suggest it. There might be a new duty that you want to take on, a new department to move to, or maybe now is the time for you to move on to someplace totally new. Whatever your goals might be, continuously reevaluate them so that at least once or twice a year you know exactly where you're going and have a written plan for getting there. Write your goals down, since writing seems to cement them and the process reveals the necessary steps to reach each goal.

Everyone is capable of doing extraordinary things if they want to. Lee Iacocca's story, from his book, *Iacocca: An Autobiography*, is proof of that.

"As you go through life there are thousands of little forks in the road, and there are a few really big forks—those moments of reckoning, moments of truth. There are times in everyone's life when something constructive is born out of adversity. There are times when things seem so bad you've got to grab your fate by the shoulders and shake it," Iacocca wrote.

"I began my life as the son of immigrant parents—nothing was ever given to me. I worked hard for all of it. Cars were all I ever cared about. I went to college and became an engineer trainee, landing a dream job at Ford. About a year later, I made a career change. I stayed at Ford, but moved from engineering into sales. I was bashful and awkward—I had no natural talent for sales. So I worked hard at it. I got another promotion and moved up to manager—my territory was dead last out of the 13 the company had. I learned, listened, found some mentors and my team started selling more. Then the company faced a major reorganization—I kept a job, but it was a demotion. I worked harder.

"At age 36, I was the general manager of the biggest division in the world's second largest company. I had bypassed 100 older and more experienced people on my way to this job. I really had fire-in-my-belly, couldn't wait to get to work each morning. I worked at developing a new product—a history maker. The results pushed me into the Vice President's chair. I thought I'd be the next president here, but they hired a guy from a competitor to take the job I longed for. Many told me to wait and see. I considered resigning—got a job offer or two. Problem was, I still loved the car business, so I stayed. The other guy only lasted 19 months. Shortly thereafter I became the President of Ford Motor Company, with a $3.5 billion payroll for 432,000 employees, with annual sales revenues of $14.9 billion. I'd made it! Then, life got complicated and I clashed with the Chairman of the Board.

"And I got fired. Fired! I lived through and learned just how terrible it was to be let go. I was 54—many thought I should just accept my fate and play golf the rest of my life. Being fired taught me a few lessons. My friends disappeared. People I'd known for decades just dropped me. The greatest shock of my life was that after I was fired, everyone deserted me.

"I did get some job offers. A lot of other businesses needed a talented leader, but cars were in my blood and I loved them. That's how I came to run Chrysler—only I didn't know it was gonna be 'Mission Impossible.' The company had problems—it seemed a tough challenge—so I took it," Iacocca stated.

"The rest is legendary—the hard work, the going to the U.S. government for a bail out loan that everybody opposed to avoid full-fledged bankruptcy, being CEO and spokesperson for Chrysler. Many people ask me about my roaring success—how'd I do it? I tell them it all goes back to what my parents taught me. Apply yourself. Get all the education you can, but then, by God, *do* something! Make something happen. It isn't easy, but if you keep your nose to the grindstone and work at it, you can become as great as you want to be."

CHAPTER 8

Get That Raise!

Carpe diem! (Seize the day!)

In a recent annual national survey, *USA Today* reported that 24% of all women workers and 20% of all male employees went to their bosses and asked for a raise. Of those, *55% of the women* and *41% of the men failed.* Learning the success formula *before* you approach your manager can greatly improve your chances of successfully achieving your goal. You won't jeopardize your career because you asked at the wrong time or, most important, in the wrong way. Those who succeed in obtaining raises have used some important strategies and guidelines to advance their careers. You are about to learn the strategies and tools you need to get a raise. Today's global marketplace means it is unlikely that raises will be automatic in the future. Most will be negotiated and based on your contributions. This is typically what is meant by "merit raise." You can influence your boss and company significantly if you understand and use some key guidelines to prepare before approaching your employer.

Here's a good case to learn from. Julie had worked as a credit manager at an electronics company for seven years but had not received a raise in two. She and her husband could barely make ends meet, so he pushed her to ask for a raise when they wanted to buy a new car. Julie was nervous but determined. Entering her boss's office on a Friday afternoon after he'd finished a long executive team meeting, Julie quickly blurted out, "I've worked for Jameson

Electronics now for seven years, but I haven't had a raise in the last two. I think being a loyal employee is worth a lot. My car is pretty old, and we want to buy a new one. Cars are expensive, you know, so I need a raise." She added that she felt $200 more a month was appropriate. Her boss asked her why she believed she deserved a raise. "Loyalty," Julie responded. "Seven years—not too many people have been here that long. I think that's significant. I've been in the credit area all that time, so I really know my stuff—and other companies are giving raises—I believe I deserve one, too."

Julie hadn't noticed her boss seemed stressed out until she heard him say, "Julie, you know that company sales are down. Today the CEO was emphatic about lowering budgets. The time isn't right for a longevity raise. Last year, at your review, we talked about your computer skills. I recommended you take those Excel and database courses. I think you would be able to improve collections if you used a more sophisticated system. You haven't taken those courses yet, so unless I see an increase in your skills, productivity, or quicker collections on your part, I cannot justify a raise. My answer at this time must be no."

This certainly wasn't the result Julie wanted. So what were her mistakes? First and foremost, she assumed longevity was enough. Longevity isn't an asset in today's marketplace, productivity is. In fact, managers often refer to Julie's approach as the "entitlement syndrome," as if it were a disease. "Needing a raise" rarely encourages employers to pay more. *Picking up new skills or going the extra mile is what most often influences employers to pay more.* Additionally, her timing and approach were poor. She didn't gauge her boss's mood. She picked the wrong day and certainly used an approach destined for failure.

Worst Ways of Asking for a Raise

- **I need the money.** Your finances are your problem—not your employer's. Never ask because you bought a car or house, are divorcing, or are having a baby. These reasons hold no bottom-line value to an employer.

- **But she got a raise!** Most bosses are infuriated by this argument. Perhaps the other employee has done a better job than you. Discussing others' salaries is unwise, often against corporate rules, and may have serious repercussions. Again, this reason doesn't say how or what you've done to merit *your* increase.

- **Threatening to quit.** More than one boss has said, "Fine. Go." Many top executives and managers think they are irreplaceable. Everyone can be replaced, so being this bold may result in losing your job, not improving it.

- **Refusing to work overtime or do new projects.** Most employers feel that this tactic demonstrates you are not a team player. You may get a small victory but quickly lose the war.

- **Whiny never works.** This little-kid approach annoys managers and puts you in a childish light. Pouting, complaining, moping, or brooding won't change the results—only positive actions will.

- **Blackmailing them with another job offer.** Some people bluff or use a job offer they don't really plan to take as a bargaining chip to get their organization to give them a raise. It's a very risky minefield that often ends with your resignation instead of a raise.

Where the Biggest Raises Come From

The absolute best way to maximize your raise is to quit your job and move to a new employer. With a "promotional raise" you get a move up—a promotion—and a significant salary increase together. My clients are living proof that this happens, and many have had their income go up 20, 30, 40, even 50%. I have seen a few clients actually double their salaries, so it is possible to make a huge move. Compare that to in-house raises that typically run from 3 to 7%. Even if you're not seeking a promotion, to a new employer you are attractive talent, and if you negotiate well, you'll find it pays off.

Wayne, a client, was a fifty-six-year-old mechanical engineer who was afraid to ask for a raise. He feared downsizing repercussions due to his age and the company's current status. Through the grapevine he heard of a good job, applied, and was offered the position. Wayne negotiated a 16% raise (to $90,000) plus better stock options.

You may find your best opportunity to get rich is to move elsewhere. For those who wish to remain with their employers, the following client examples outline clearly what's necessary to succeed in your quest for a raise.

The Secrets of Getting That Raise

Ken, a purchasing manager at a large manufacturing company, came to me for help in asking his boss for a raise. We discussed why he felt he deserved to be paid more. During his two-year tenure, he had made significant contributions. He'd improved the system and computerized numerous processes, making everything more user-friendly, efficient, and faster. He renegotiated several vendor contracts, securing better deals than existed before.

Additionally, he had noticed his department received over a thousand invoices per week, and there was no cross-check system with the receiving department, resulting in overpaying and double paying. Ken solved the problem using a team approach, working closely with both the receiving department and the

MIS people. This sped up the payment process to within ten days, allowing the company to take advantage of a 5% prompt payment discount that Ken had negotiated with the vendors. When I asked exactly how much that saved, he didn't know. I suggested he find out, as it could be a valuable piece of ammunition for his raise request (and it was—a savings of $98,000 over ten months!).

Another key strategy was to prepare a Hiring Chart. Here's the one Ken and I created:

KEN'S HIRING CHART	
Needs	**Contributions**
Purchasing processes and systems	• Learned advanced Excel, Access, and FoxPro. • Rewrote invoice process to simplify and computerize data. Results: Saved 10 minutes per invoice. • Created negotiations deal analysis model. Input each contract as it comes up for renewal. Obtain new bids. Negotiate better terms. Results: Reduced freight and warehouse charges, saved $12,700 (annually). • Negotiated 5% discount on bills paid within 20 days of receiving shipment (see below). • Competitive bidding reduced materials fees while maintaining quality with 25 top vendors, including

Needs	Contributions
Reorganized the entire receiving/ invoice ordering/payment process	Amoco, Simpson, Glenn Steel, Mitsubishi, and Todd. Savings from 1/01 to 1/02 was $1.2 million. • Organized a committee with accounting and receiving. • Developed new plan to improve process time to immediate retrieval, verification of received goods, and authorization of payment. • Worked with the programming department to develop computerized, fast, and easy system. Beta-tested system with Amoco deliveries. Worked out bugs and safeguards to avoid double payments and minimize employee theft. Implemented entire system conversion 3 months after first group meeting. Results: • Saved 10 hours per week in accounting. • Speedy check-in caused no slowdowns in receiving. • Obtained 5% discount in 90% of cases (incorrect shipments account for most of the remaining 10%).

Needs	Contributions
	• Total savings during 10 months of implementation (1 month with Amoco, 9 months with 20 other vendors) = $98,972. • Projected savings over next two years with full vendor participation estimated at $237,532.

We also discussed, at length, the necessity of waiting until his manager was in a good mood to insure he'd be more receptive to the proposed raise. Ken had prepared a persuasive argument illustrated by his Hiring Chart. Ken met with his boss, who asked for time to think about his request, considering the company's budgets were really tight. Getting back to Ken a few days later, his supervisor told him, "You are doing a great job here. We can give you a little bonus now, $3,000, based on all the systems improvements. The new fiscal year starts in three months, and at your current pay step we have little room for any raise. I worked with HR and we'll move you into the next manager tier beginning on July 1. That'll bring a $7,000 increase, so you'll be at $63,000 plus the new title. I feel you've done an outstanding job, Ken, and this is long overdue."

Ken had really done his homework. He also presented his case with facts on his performance and quantified his value to his employer. At the time he got this promotion, the company's policy was to hold tight on raises. Ken's presentation enabled his boss to reclassify his job, to a higher classification, thus moving him up the personnel stepladder to give him a raise he had truly earned.

There's another avenue you could pursue to obtain a raise, as this client did. Deanna really liked her job and all the responsibilities she undertook. Her employer was a nonprofit whose cause she believed in. Yet over the past year, she felt that her employer had taken advantage of her. She admitted that she was to blame because she took on extra work. She told me, "The association has doubled in the five years that I've been with them. I love the job, but it seems everyone keeps giving me more to do. I now oversee the major fundraiser, plus a dozen smaller specialty events, recruit all the volunteers, develop the sponsorships for both my projects and other fundraising events, plus I produce our quarterly newsletter."

I asked how these duties differed from those she had when she first started. Deanna said, "Well, five years ago, I was hired to coordinate our two major fundraising events."

I smiled and told her, "You've just revealed the best strategy of all to obtain a raise. Your job description has changed entirely during the last few years. You've taken on more responsibility and have contributed a great deal more than when you started. Many organizations tend to simply accept these contributions without increasing the base salary. I think you can make a strong case for a raise and still remain in your organization. If I hear you correctly, you don't sound as if you really want to move on."

Deanna immediately responded, "But they won't give me a raise. John [her boss] will say what he always says: 'If you want a lot of money, move to the corporate sector. We are a charity, and funds for administration and staff are strained as it is.' Believe me, we've all heard him say that on numerous occasions." I told her we could present a strong case, if she wanted to try, and outlined our strategy. "You and I could create a performance chart that shows your old job description, the new one, and highlight some of the major contributions you've made. You will also need to go to the library and research competitive salary surveys. We need that information to make the pitch. Last, we'd need to role-play your conversation with John and work on how to deal with his objections. You'll need good answers to 'Nobody's getting a raise' and his standard reply of 'Go to a corporation.'"

Deanna decided to put in the effort. She called her association and got a good current salary survey. She dug out her original job description, and we created the new one based on all the duties she was currently performing (see charts she used). She worked hard on role-playing—dealing with objections or any kind of conflict wasn't easy for her. In her meeting with John, Deanna pointed out all the new responsibilities she'd taken on, suggesting her program coordinator job really fell into the manager level. She reiterated that her duties had actually doubled without a corresponding realignment of job title. Deanna's boss asked to think it over and returned the next day with his answer. He said, "Deanna, I discussed this with Mary [chairman of the board], and we both feel you are a valued and worthy employee. We have no budgets for a raise, so there will be no raise. I want us to be clear on that. We do, however, see your point that the job has changed. We decided to restructure the position and change the title to program manager. That job will hold a salary $6,000 higher than your current one, and your new position starts on the first. Congratulations."

It did indeed prove "impossible" to give Deanna a raise. Her boss's idea—a new job title—was essential to deal with the current policy. Deanna had never been more proud of herself than she was at that moment. *She got the promotion and a raise!* She also used two strategies that worked well with John—the job duties comparison charts, plus the salary surveys. Additionally, she presented a strong argument that if she wasn't there, the company would pay outside fees, since the employee likely to take her job would lack some of her acquired skills. Her "persuasion" got her exactly what she had earned and wanted.

To summarize, the success formula when asking for a raise includes the following:

- **Pick your time wisely.** Be sure to pick a time when your boss is likely to be receptive and more positive.

DEANNA'S PERFORMANCE CHART		
Old	**New**	**Contributions**
3/4 time position—organized and coordinated all aspects of the two major spring and fall fundraisers.	Coordinates all aspects of fall and spring major fundraisers, including sponsorship, marketing, and volunteer recruitment.	• Events raised $251,000 first year on job. *Last year, raised $727,000* plus $45,000 in sponsor-paid administration for a total of *$772,000.*
Full-time position—coordinator of the monthly chapter events.	Coordinates the monthly chapter meetings and hires speakers.	• Attendance was 30–40 per event when employment began. Current attendance averages 100–125 and includes luncheon and speaker. • Secured 100–150 people to work at events during the last year.
	Recruits volunteers for all association events.	• Recruited sponsors to cover funding costs. Secured free printing, hotel sites, and prizes for all association programs. Approximate value for last two years $110,000.

Old	New	Contributions
	Heads the entire corporate sponsorship program. Publishes quarterly newsletter.	• Newsletter campaign raised $26,000 in 5 issues we've mailed and publicizes upcoming and special events without extra costs.

- *Do your homework.* Research your organization's policies and step grades. Look into whether or not your duties can be reclassified. Obtain industry salary surveys to support and validate your request.

- *Quantify your request.* Use salary surveys and job comparisons to support your suggested compensation level.

- *Provide proof.* Charts can be very persuasive. Use either the hiring chart or the performance chart to illustrate your growth, achievement, and depth of contribution.

- *Practice your pitch.* Role-play your request with a colleague or friend. Go over it several times until you are cool and comfortable with the request.

- *Overcome objections.* Identify the potential objections you think your boss is likely to make and prepare solid answers. Then practice dealing effectively with the objections.

- *Know your boss.* Adjust your request to his or her personality and operations style.

- **Remain positive.** Expect that your boss will need to either think about your request or discuss it with upper management. Don't push it if there's no immediate response.

- **Tolerate silence.** People often are quiet when they are contemplating. Don't babble—wait for your boss to absorb what you are saying.

- **Convince yourself.** Know your value and worth. You must be confident to be effective in your persuasion.

When the Answer Is No

Not every single salary request gets approved, no matter how fabulous you are on the job. The big question to answer is why your raise request was rejected. Your performance may deserve it, your efforts may warrant it, your accomplishments may support it, but still the answer is no. There are times when the best persuasion skills will not move the mountain. If you've been rejected, consider these possible factors and act accordingly:

1. Ask what it will take to get a raise. Get the specifics from your boss so you have a clear idea of what you need to do. Clarify in writing what was discussed, so you can pursue your raise request once you have achieved the specifics. A written memo is a great reminder once you've achieved the goal, particularly if it involves acquiring a new skill or skills. This is a key step to determine if the boss is being truthful, helpful, or maybe just doesn't like you. It is best to be clear on what skill(s) or work needs to be accomplished—or whether working for someone else might be a better (and richer) alternative.

2. Accept that your current salary is all the job is worth. When an employer evaluates the job, he or she often dictates the maxi-

mum that particular job is worth. The employer will pay no more—willing to replace the worker rather than up the compensation to get those tasks done. To make more, you'll need to take on new tasks (inquire if that's an option) or move on to a new job with a new employer.

3. **Know that small employers tend to pay less.** Profits and gross income are typically less in small organizations. There may be limited budgets to absorb the overhead increase a raise will cost. These small employers would pay more if they could, but the reality is they can't afford to.

4. **Understand priorities.** The company's goals and agenda may be in using dollars for equipment or facility improvements instead of retaining talent with better salaries. They may have chosen to retain benefits, often absorbing their significant increases in order to keep them.

As you ponder your company's refusal to pay you more, keep these two solutions in mind:

- **Keep producing results.** The company knows what you want and is watching. If you continue to perform and maximize your contributions, you *may* be rewarded down the line. Do expand your internal network. Volunteer to be on key committees with upper management. Also volunteer to work on those projects viewed as important high priorities by the company's top executives.

- **You can always get another job.** This is your ace in the hole. You can choose to move on. In my experience, most people land the biggest salary increases when they move to a new company. That is always an option for you.

CHAPTER 9

Moving Your Business to the Next Level

Think little goals and expect
small achievements. Think *big* goals
and achieve giant successes.

—RR

You're a business owner and you want to renew, revitalize, change, and, most of all, improve your business. I adhere to the trusted adage "Work smarter, not harder." If you're reading this you probably agree with that wholeheartedly.

Running a business is exciting, thrilling, financially rewarding, challenging, and exhausting. The initial passion can get lost in the stress and strain of running the business. It can be a dangerous path for those who flirt with burnout.

Mark LeBlanc, author of *Grow Your Business* (Beaver's Pond Press, 2000: www.smallbusinesssuccess.com), warned business owners, "You have to avoid self-destruction. You are close to burnout if you run at a pace of eighty to ninety hours per week. When a life event occurs, such as marital problems/divorce or an illness, you'll crash and burn out. The pace allows for full speed ahead for only so long. It's better to set a long-term doable pace—sixty-five hours a week, with a three-day weekend every thirty days. You must create the maximum hours per week limit and force yourself to live by it.

"Many service professionals—doctors, dentists, consultants—are driven by a need to succeed to the exclusion of all else. That stubborn drive can put blinders on you, eliminating the options to have a fuller life," LeBlanc noted.

The road for a business owner evolves and changes. The push to work smarter, not harder, is something we all strive for. The "smarter way" for me is working less and getting paid more. This chapter focuses completely on that goal.

Many solutions for learning new skills or solving business problems are readily available. Expert problem solving for every conceivable subject is within your grasp—just reach for a book.

Everyone can benefit from reading. Training your mind by acquiring knowledge through reading books, articles, journals, and the like—this is a powerful success strategy that can be used in any venture to broaden your knowledge and expertise, as well as enrich your wallet.

Getting Business to Come to You

How many times have you thought, "Okay, here's the deal—the big kahuna—this one's gonna make me rich, or famous, or both"? Many business owners are looking for the big kahuna. That's all they need to slam-dunk their business to megasuccess. While no single event will likely make or break you, consistent performance will keep your bills paid and your salary high. It's hitting singles and doubles—small as they may be, they add up to bigger monthly revenues. Every once in a while you'll hit a home run, maybe even a grand slam—but it's the constant single hits that keep most businesses prosperous.

If you own a business, the choices are yours. You can have a consistent game plan, one that adapts and grows revenues. You set the fees and standards for customer service, you control purchasing and marketing. You make the rules, set the hours, and run your operation. That means you change it, improve it, enhance it.

If you're looking to move ahead and want a larger and more consistent stream of revenue, these four things can assist you in getting more business:

1. More effective marketing strategies.
2. Positive publicity.
3. More free time to make more $$$.
4. Controlled losses, restructured fees and prices.

Top business owners who run multimillion-dollar organizations operate from a just-do-it-and-get-it-done attitude. You need to, too.

More Effective Marketing Strategies

Most marketing works, but some works better than others, especially once you have an established business. There are a few strategies—trade shows, public speaking, websites—that can be powerful tools.

Trade Shows

"Trade shows are the purest form of business competition," said marketing guru Steve Miller, author of *How to Get the Most Out of Trade Shows* (NTC Business Books, 2000). "You must establish a brand and attract attention—if you don't want to use your creative resources to do that, then you better stay home."

Don't get stuck in the "I need more customers" trap. Earn more from the customers you already have, Miller warned. "The best source of new revenue is from current customers. You simply need to offer the customers you already have more services and products that are valuable to them. The key—get to know your customers and their needs well."

Miller offered these tips for success when you participate in a trade show:

1. Pick the right show. To find it, ask customers what shows they go to.
2. Know exactly what you expect from the show (number of leads, amount of sales).
3. Don't confuse being busy with effectiveness.
4. Make your booth talk to your market. Who are you? What do you do? It's a big mistake not to have any signs or displays. Why would anyone want to stop and talk to you?
5. Meet people. If you won't make the creative effort to stand out and greet potential customers, stay home.

Trade shows may not be right for your business. The fact is, most people forget to consider market trends and expand or change their services or products. A key strategy for success is to sell more to the customers you already have. So take a few minutes to think about your current customers, their buying needs, and whether you can offer them more services or products. List three ways to get your current customers to spend more with you. What can you enhance, add to, or create that will increase your average sale? Test and implement these ideas as soon as possible.

Public Speaking

Marketing with speeches and seminars can be a good way to attract clients or customers. Eventually you can get paid to get up and speak. Speeches have definitely been a major source of new clients for me, as well as for many other consultants, accountants, doctors, lawyers, and service professionals. I find I attract high-quality clients this way, too. It does take time to develop a speech or seminar, but once done, you can offer it at the local library, community center, college, continuing education center, and so on. The hosting organization pays to advertise the event, and you simply show up to do the seminar. If people like your speech, some will buy your products or services. Although your first speeches may be free, the next step is to charge an honorarium (always ask for one) of anywhere from $100 to $500. Accomplished speakers can earn between $500 and $2,500 for one speech. Professionals can earn up to $10,000, but those folks are usually celebrities or recognized experts in their fields, with years of success behind them.

Variety is not necessarily the spice of life in the seminar business. Develop one or two speeches and perfect them until they are well done and well received. Use them repeatedly—repetition uses your time most efficiently, and it also allows you to improve delivery. The topic must be one of interest to you *and* be something potential clients want to know more about.

For example, Dr. Anderson, a chiropractor, built an entire practice on nutritional seminars. He sold some products—vitamins, booklets—but his real goal was to turn attendees into patients. He found that usually 20–30% of his audience members became long-term patients who referred family members and others. He gave one speech a week and used this technique to build his chiropractic business into one of the largest in Kansas City. He still does at least one or two speeches a month—it's the most cost-effective advertising he's done. He's tried advertising on TV, on radio, and in newspapers. He's tried coupons and discounts. Nothing works as well as his speeches to bring in high-quality business.

You'll need to do some research to select your best topic, since it needs to meet an important criterion. Writing a speech or putting together a workshop can be time-consuming. So pick a subject that can be repeated often. Time-sensitive subjects, such as making Christmas wreaths might be a big winner in November but will be useless during the ten other months of the year. It's safer to select "Financial Planning to Retire by Fifty" and then use it over and over again.

Catchy titles and compelling course descriptions are an essential part of your success plan. You won't succeed without them. My topics—"The Hidden Job Market" and "60 Seconds & You're Hired!—never failed to draw big crowds.

Advertising potential benefits from a seminar is one thing, but delivering them is critical for succeeding. Good speakers provide plenty of substance. They are entertaining, interesting to listen to, mix in a bit of audience interaction, and are careful not to be too academic. By that I mean they don't try to cram too much information into the allotted time.

Miriam Otte, author of *Marketing with Speeches and Seminars* (Zest Press, 1998), cautioned new speakers on common errors: "People will pay for programs, but they must offer specific benefits to the buyer attending, like how to do something better. This can be a challenge to folks who know a great deal on a topic. They are tempted to 'data dump,' instead of keeping a narrow focus that is specific and of interest to their audience. New speakers also tend to forget that what is commonplace to the speaker might seem like rocket science when it's new to others." Craft a speech carefully, then decide what to put in and what to leave out, she noted.

Nothing will take the place of practicing and trying your material. Otte recommended, "Teach it, then fine-tune it. Most top speakers sound as though they are ad-libbing—jokes, no notes—but in fact they have tried and tested every single part of their speech. They know how it works 'cause they've said it before—many times, in fact. Practice does make perfect."

Content is always of paramount importance—good substance is essential. But how you say it is also important. You must develop good presentation skills if you plan to use your speeches to attract clients. Work on one speech until you've really mastered it—both the content and your delivery. Then sell it and resell it, using it over and over again. To gain experience in public speaking, take a class, join Toastmasters, and/or hire a coach to help you improve your presentation.

Additionally, you must stay current in order to make your seminar *feel* current. Read books, especially all the classics on your topic. Go to other seminars and see how competitors or colleagues run their programs. You can learn a lot from watching others. The more knowledgeable you are, the easier it'll be to discuss the topic and answer audience questions.

Speeches are a terrific opportunity to sell your products and services. There is a fine line between mentioning your services or products while on the stage and pushing to sell them. Hard sells turn people off. It often revolts buyers. The county fair hard sell might work for knives, but it will not build long-term, repeat business for you. On the other hand, not mentioning your services is a waste of a golden opportunity. An easy solution is to have someone else introduce you and have them describe your product, book, or services.

Always have a flyer on your services, and give one to everyone who attends. The best strategy for doing this is to create handouts or materials you'll cover in class and staple your flyer to them. People keep the handouts, and you'll be amazed by how many call even years after you've given the speech. I wouldn't have believed it, but I do get calls *years* after people heard my speeches, so always include a phone number, email address, or website address that is long term and permanent.

A mailing list is a gold mine. Savvy speakers are always adding to their list. You need to create a mailing list, too, so always get attendees' addresses and emails. When speaking for an association or group, ask organizers for them. Or offer a free email article and ask attendees to provide their addresses to get it. Many people and organizations sell their mailing lists, which can be enormously useful when you are trying to pump up business.

Long term, these people are all "hot prospects" who have already met you and can be marketed to over time to buy and rebuy whatever you have to sell. Put their names into a database—it's your moneymaking machine, so work it actively by sending out informational articles, ads, and seminar notices. Old clients tell others, so always let them know where and when you are giving a speech.

Email marketing is quickly replacing direct mail for two reasons—it's free and it works. At a recent seminar, I asked the audience how they heard about it. I was astounded to find that out of the 150 people in attendance, only a handful saw a local newspaper article written about me. More than 75 people came because of the email they received on the program. Use email to market, inform, and send tips—your business will grow, and so will your profits.

The next part of this strategy is to determine exactly where to speak. The easiest programs are the ones you arrange to give through continuing education departments, local associations, groups, colleges, or clubs. Many allow you the option of offering your seminar quarterly or even monthly. Finding a few places and offering your seminar more frequently is the ideal, as it's less work for you. Typically they do the mailing (which you should augment) and you teach the class. Add to any advertising a group does for your upcoming speech by sending out your own flyers and emails to your mailing list and the media.

Be sure to get a few testimonials stating how valuable your program is to use in marketing to clients for future speeches.

To summarize, follow the four rules for success in using seminars and speeches to attract customers:

Rule 1 Pick a topic you love, one you can share with others. Select a subject with a long life span and become an expert on it.

Rule 2 Use a catchy title and an alluring description, and deliver more than you promise. Offer testimonials on the value of your program. These endorsements will result in more attendees and higher product or service sales. Create handouts with nice front covers listing your name, address, phone number, and website and email addresses, and include a flyer on your products and services as part of the handout (usually the last page).

Rule 3 Give one great speech, repeatedly. It will attract more clients and save you work.

Rule 4 Build a mailing list.

On Becoming an Authority

Credibility and credentials. Most speakers and consultants need to build credentials and offer reasons why they are worth listening to. The very best way to do this is to become a published author. It's not the easiest way, but it's by far the most effective. You could, for instance, author an article that gets published on a website. Look for sites and offer your work for free, in exchange for a link to your website. You could also call and suggest a topic to a local business journal or small newspaper editor. Ask if you can write a "spec" article, which they can run if they like it. Be sure you know what the paper's ideal article length is, and know exactly what topic and angle you plan to write about *before* you call.

Other places to get your articles published include association and professional journals, newsletters, and magazines. Of course, the best way to get publicity through writing is to graduate and write a regular column. The most prestigious and effective tool for long-term career building, though, is to actually write a book—one you can use as your calling card and sell at your seminars and speeches. Additionally, you can create a workbook, manual, resource guide, or booklet to sell. These products require a time investment, but once created they can be sold and resold. For a small investment, you could record an audiocassette on your topic, be it motivational or informational (both is best), and sell that. All of these ideas will add to your credibility and build your name as an expert on the subject, which is the *true* goal.

Don't misunderstand: many professionals and consultants sell other people's books, tapes, and products at their seminars. Some create their own tapes and sell them. That's wise and can be profitable. But to really carve out your niche, *you* need to consider taking this step to move *your* business up to the next level. *As the author of a book, you can charge higher fees, both as a speaker and as a consultant or service provider.*

Writing a book is a labor of love—it's a major endeavor! The road from concept to published product is long. It's a part of your long-term, not short-term, plan. Many authors will tell you it took them a long while to learn the publishing process—like the fact that authors first write book proposals and then approach publishers, before ever writing their books. Publishers often change the original idea a great deal. They want to know who your target audience is and require a marketing plan explaining exactly how you'll reach the book's intended readers.

This is my sixth book, and all my books required well-crafted, lengthy book proposals to sell them to publishers. In fact, my first book idea was about the job search process; it was rejected by every publisher I sent it to. But I did get two different publishers talking to me, and one suggested I write about interviewing—that's how my first book, *60 Seconds & You're Hired!*, was born. I based the book on my seminar and used the class outline as my table of contents. That made the book easier to write. Writing a book and getting it published can take eighteen months to two years or longer, but nothing will enhance your career like becoming an author. You'll attract more business with more to sell and cross-sell—your published work can and will move you ahead, producing higher revenues as a result.

Henriette Anne Klauser, author of *Write It Down, Make It*

Happen (Fireside, 2000), coaches people who want to write and get a book published. She shared this story of one client's success: "I believe that people can write a book if they get the proper guidance and have someone who acts as their cheerleader, believing they can do it. Most books enhance your income, as it's a credential, showing you are an authority on a subject. One client, who reflected on the process of taking him through the steps to write a book proposal, calls it 'his million-dollar assignment,' because—since his book was released—he's earned over a million dollars. Not off his book sales—those have been modest—but from being a published authority, allowing him to secure more business, with higher fees being paid for his consulting, his seminars, and other services."

Whether it's a booklet, audiotape, article, or book, getting published is an effective strategy for advancing your business. They become your calling cards and often attract new business to you as a result.

Make Money Off Your Website

Not every business needs a website. Many businesses that do have sites don't generate sales income, either. That's a mistake. Your website can be a little gold mine.

In the future, more and more business will be generated from the Internet, opening up new ways to both market and create revenues for your company.

Rich Christiano, president of Christiano Film Group, showed how's he's grown his business—a business employing himself and one part-time staff person—to $700,000 in annual revenues.

Rich incorporated some very smart marketing techniques to push his business over the top. His business consists of selling videos of his six Christian movies and fifty different videos produced by other people. He found by adding "partner" products, he could increase his sales and profits dramatically.

Rich said the secret of his success was his website, which is now his most effective way to market and sell to his customers.

"I used to get 5% of my business from the website. Last year, we changed that," he said. "The single thing we did was add a shopping cart to our site. People used to have to call us to order—now it's direct. The nice thing is it's superefficient—we get the order and ship it. Clean and fast. Our phone bills went down, staff time went down, so we profited more. We are currently getting 30% of our business off our site, and it's growing weekly. I highly recommend having your website equipped with a shopping cart to purchase books, tapes, and/or other products directly from you. If you don't want to hassle with the mailings, hire someone to do it for you."

When Rich secured a deal to air his films on TV, it was the small ad at the end of the program—"To order, visit our website at www.christianmovies.com"—that really pumped up the sales. Prior to that, he used a toll-free number service that charged him $5 per order. Now he lists a phone number that's not toll-free and his website. Rich commented: "As your business grows, you've got to watch costs and trends. The Web is where it's at; it's free, and that's where the people are." It's always a good idea, though, to list a website, phone, and fax, giving people as many ways as possible to find and buy your product or service.

Rich noted he gained a big savings from dropping some direct mail, which cost several thousand dollars per postal mailing. Instead, he switched to email campaigns. When he gets a Web order, he sends a thank-you email telling the customer he or she is now also signed up to receive newsletters and specials on featured films. Rich advised: "Collect email addresses. Don't expect them to just sign up, do it for them, whether you've met them at a speech, online, or on the phone. Email newsletters are a far better way to stay in touch with your customer base at no expense. Your sales go up, and profits go up, too. The newsletter needs to be one of substance, with an offer to buy something. In my case, it's a featured film we've discounted. Yours can be a

Advertising Response Rate

Permission emails (e-newsletters, okayed ads, etc.): 11.5%
Traditional postal direct mail: 1 to 1.5%
Banners: .055%

Source: Business 2.0

book or any product, for that matter. Keep the newsletter 'newsy.' If it's too long, no one wants to read it, and if it's just an ad, it gets ignored, too. The secret is to offer news, reviews, tips—something worth reading."

Michael Davis, marketing website consultant for Quik Internet, echoed my belief that your website needs to be a business in and of itself, producing a revenue stream. "Making your site a great brochure—the old way to use the Web—doesn't generate direct income. The new marketing strategy is to drive sales to your site to sell your services or products. The costs to look legitimate and professional have decreased dramatically, enabling small businesses to create their own snappy websites for less than $1,500."

Your website needs to advertise you, your services, and your product. Today, many people will go to your website, which is quickly replacing mailing out slick flyers. For more specifics on adding to your site and building traffic, visit www.websitesuccess.net.

To add to your resumé stream, team up with others to sell their products. Amazon.com lets you set up an affiliate site and pays you a small percentage of any book orders from your site. Barnesandnoble.com does the same. Don't have products, or don't have enough? Rich sells his own products and represents many others. He strikes deals with producers—both he and the producer profit from a sale—so it's a win-win situation for both.

Marketing guru and author Steve Miller recommended becoming an affiliate or associate with Amazon.com and creating a link to Amazon, from which you receive a referral fee for all the sales that come through your site. "This is free money," Miller said. "Just pick ten to twenty good books and place them on your site with the appropriate link to Amazon. It's unbelievably easy to do, and once there, all you do is collect a check—we're getting a few hundred dollars a month from this program."

I know this works for several people who list all my books on their site and have reported back that they are great sellers. Small and large businesses do this as a service to their customers. The Amazon link is so easy that once you set it up you literally do nothing and they mail you, the business owner, a check. That's the kind of passive revenue stream I like. It works while you sleep, eat, or play.

Look around and partner with other sites—try to arrange for links that drive traffic to your site and produce more sales and revenues for you. Today, the cheapest way to build a business is through email newsletters and online advertising. And it works, too!

Publicity—How to Get Your Name in the News

One day I had a new assistant, Kim, handling our phones, and Dawnelle, my executive assistant, was working on the computer. I walked into the office and Kim said, after retrieving our voice mail, "Terry Goulder called."

She never got another word out. Dawnelle and I looked at each other for one moment of shock and then began to scream, yell, and jump up and down for about three minutes. Finally I said, "Wait, wait—what did he want?"

Kim replied, smiling, "To talk about having you on the show. Obviously you know who he is."

Sure did—Terry Goulder was a producer for *Oprah,* the *big* national show for an author to appear on. I was thrilled, excited, exuberant, ecstatic. A big *wow!*

The first times are the most exciting—they will be for you, too. It's a thrill to have the world listen to you. But the benefits—the sales, the new clients, the business growth—that's why you should be excited. Nothing helps your business like great publicity. Being on *Oprah* has generated thousands of book sales for many authors.

Gene, a big-city restaurant owner, reported this success. "I was totally shocked when the Seattle newspaper reviewed my restaurant and put it on their 'Top 10 Restaurants' list for the year. Our business quadrupled overnight, and it's stayed strong ever since. Of course, we continuously promote that we were on that list to maximize the long-term benefits. It's been over two years and we keep growing and getting new customers."

Business owners, experts, professionals—publicity can do more than any advertisement could. You probably know many other people who have publicity success stories, so how do you learn to use publicity to aid you and grow your business?

Publicity begets more publicity, but a common misconception about media exposure is that one article will make you rich and famous. It will not. But consistent publicity can—getting your name in the news *a lot* will add to your credibility, increase your sales, and bring in the dollars. So how do you generate that kind of name-making credibility? A common mistake is to ask the media to write about your business. Randall, owner of a retail store, asked me, "How did you get the local newspaper to write that great article about you? I asked the editor to write about me, and he said no." They said no because Randall didn't learn the rules of this game before he asked. If he really wanted to get publicity, he needed to *create news* involving himself or his business. You can hire an agency or PR consultant or, if you plan to do this often, learn to think of "news hooks" yourself. To get publicity, you have to learn the rules of dealing with the media.

First, you always need news hooks—the angle for a story you suggest or "pitch," as the PR people say, in a press release. The news angle must contain something of interest to the news outlet's audience. No matter what your business is, something about it is newsworthy—usually something basic about what you do. Maybe there's a new trend or new angle on an old story or something linked to a holiday. Anything can get you noticed. There's a couple in Seattle who write love letters to each other every single day of their fifty-plus-year marriage. Come Valentine's Day, this couple is on TV, radio, and in all the papers—now *that's* linking the angle (daily love letters) to a holiday (Valentine's Day).

Many people are mystified by the idea of writing a press release. Read a couple of publicity books and then write and test your release. You could pay someone to write it for you. But you can and should learn how to do this yourself. Since people find getting started difficult, I've included a press release I wrote and used repeatedly to generate hundreds of media engagements on TV and radio or to get interviews for magazines and newspaper articles.

You'll notice I've quoted myself as if a reporter had interviewed me for an article. That's a secret technique—create a release with quotes and usable tips from you. I have had this exact article reprinted in several newspapers, just as I wrote it. That's the key—write the release as if it were an article. That makes it easy for the editor to cut and use it "as is."

Joan Stewart, a former newspaper editor and PR consultant who runs www.publicityhound.com, explained, "The media has rules and you need to understand those rules. There are different rules for print (newspapers and magazines) and another set for TV or radio. The key mistake people make is to not learn the rules, thinking, 'How can the media help me?' The right question to ask yourself is 'How can I help the media?' and ultimately help yourself. People start by going after the big

SAMPLE PRESS RELEASE

You Can Land a Job in Just 60 Seconds

Savvy job hunters using a new hiring strategy are finding that landing a job is a snap. Many are obtaining dream positions while other people haven't gotten to first base yet. What's their secret? "They are using the 60 Second Sell," says best-selling author *Robin Ryan,* a frequent lecturer whose technique is outlined in her newest book *60 Seconds & You're Hired!* (Penguin, 2000).

"Employers make snap decisions," says Ryan. "They scan and reject resumés in twenty seconds. In the interview, candidates must effectively sell themselves in just one minute or someone else will get the job." Ryan has advised job hunters for years to use her technique, and many report it to be the most influential job tool they've ever used. "Employers only remember a few things about a candidate after the interview," says Ryan. "Using the 60 Second Sell focuses the employer's attention toward remembering a candidate's most important attributes. To create your 60 Second Sell, analyze the job duties the employer wants accomplished and then select your top five selling points—your strongest abilities to do the job. Link these five points together using a few sentences that can be spoken in sixty seconds. This is your 60 Second Sell." Ryan recommends that job hunters use this tool early in the interview to answer the opening question of "Tell me about yourself." The 60 Second Sell is also the perfect way to close an interview, leaving your strongest reasons for being able to do the job fresh in the employer's mind as you depart.

In *60 Seconds & You're Hired!* Ryan teaches this trademark technique, plus offers advice on other ways that job hunters can succeed in an interview, most notably:

- *Prepare thoroughly for the interview.* Research the employer's needs, and prepare examples of how you've done that kind of work in the past. Computer and communication skills are traits that rank high on employers' list.

- *Prepare a list of questions to ask the employer.* Cover job duties and management styles, but avoid asking about salary or benefits. Job duty questions impress employers, showing that you are really interested in their job. Display enthusiasm by maintaining eye contact and smiling—nonverbal behavior counts for a lot.
- *Practice answering questions in advance, and answer each question in less than sixty seconds.* To engage employers, job hunters must be positive and concise and demonstrate their abilities in less than sixty seconds. This takes practice, as does answering questions like "What is your greatest weakness?" or "Tell me about a coworker you didn't like or work well with."
- *Salary is important, so negotiate the entire package up front.* The biggest salary increases come from quitting a job and moving to a new employer. With employers facing shortages getting even $1 more per hour adds up. Once the position and salary are offered, Ryan suggests that candidates ask if the employer can do better. Amazingly, this simple question often results in an instant increase.

Robin Ryan is a Seattle career counselor, national speaker, and bestselling author of *60 Seconds & You're Hired!*, *Winning Cover Letters*, and *Winning Resumés*. She's appeared on over five thousand TV and radio shows, including *Oprah*, *NBC Nightly News*, and *CNN*, plus she writes a weekly column for the *Seattle Times*. Her online columns are syndicated to *USAToday.com, and CNN.com*. She is constantly quoted in magazines and newspapers, including *Money*, *Newsweek*, *USAToday*, *Business Week*, *Cosmopolitan*, *Woman's Day*, *The Wall Street Journal*, and *The New York Times*.

Contact Robin Ryan at her Seattle office, (425) 226-0414
email: robinryan@aol.com
Website: www.robinryan.com

guns—the *Today* show, *Oprah,* the big daily newspapers. The best place to start is with smaller local papers and magazines, where being 'local' is newsworthy, and then build to bigger media after catching some publicity with the smaller fish."

Sound Bites

Popular experts and sought-after authors all know it's essential to have a few good sound bites to offer the media when the opportunity of an interview arises. Joyce Taylor, a popular Seattle TV anchor, revealed the secret behind why the media wants sound bites: "Television is a powerful medium, where you have a short amount of time to get a message across. A great sound bite conveys the concise message in the fewest words possible. It's even better if the sound bite is an interesting fact, such as '85% of all jobs are not advertised.' That catches attention and helps make the story the reporter is trying to tell."

In fact, that's an actual sound bite I've used when interviewed by Ms. Taylor on KIRO-TV's *Noon Show.* I always have a few sound bites prepared before a TV or radio show. One radio host shared with me this tip on sound bites: "A great guest writes a few great sound bites before an interview or a show. She then skillfully uses them on the air to help herself be an interesting and memorable guest."

Interesting and memorable—that's what the media wants. You need to be credible, too, if you want to be seen as an authority. Let me share with you twenty-one secrets I've developed over the years for getting media coverage. These secrets have led to my being on more than seven hundred TV and radio shows and being quoted in most major newspapers and magazines. I've appeared regularly for nearly six years on CBS-affiliate KIRO-TV's *Noon News,* and as a regular expert on KIRO Radio's *Money Advice* and on Seattle's KOMO Radio *Morning Show* for seven years. Here's what I've learned.

Robin Ryan's 21 Secrets for Getting Great Media Coverage

1. Be available whenever and wherever the media needs you. Drop everything else and help reporters immediately when they call, or they'll find someone else who will.
2. Be a great resource for facts and information.
3. Be able to discuss the topic clearly so anyone can understand it.
4. Be knowledgeable, but personable and interesting, too.
5. Work on improving your "on air" presentation to appear smooth, polished, poised, relaxed, and comfortable on air.
6. Supply a list of sample questions to the TV or radio producer one day prior to the show, to insure the host asks appropriate questions. Hosts almost always ask all these sample questions. Providing your five to ten questions makes for a smoother-running and more interesting show, tailored to what you want to talk about. Left to their own devices, hosts ask bizarre questions—this step almost always assures you'll have a good interview and you'll look, and sound, great. This also is a good way to provide your phone number and Web address, so the host can read them out over the air without making mistakes.
7. Confirm time, date, location, studio phone numbers, and information about your credentials, book, website, phone number, and so forth, the day before the TV or radio show is scheduled to air or tape.
8. For radio—bring a cheat sheet with notes on major points you want to make (including sound bites) so you can answer questions, and a short bio that the host can use to promote your book, website, seminar, or business.
9. For TV—buy an outfit or suit that looks great on TV, a good solid color, nothing printed or distracting. Learn to do your

own makeup and hair—never wait or hope for the station to do it. Men need to be careful about relaxing too much—nothing looks worse than leaning back in your seat so that a big white shirt belly is all viewers notice.

10. Develop a media-friendly website. Have articles, quotes, and information ready to help the media see you as a credible and newsworthy source.

11. Tie in local angles to press releases—for example, "Robin Ryan, author of *60 Seconds & You're Hired!*, to speak at local university." Local ties make you newsworthy and will definitely up your chances of getting coverage.

12. Mail press releases to specific people, and get correct names. For print, mail your release to the appropriate editor (business editor for a business story, the features editor for lifestyle subjects, and so on). For TV news, send it to the news director at each station and to the producers of each of the station's daily shows (for instance, the *Morning News* producer and the 5:00 *News* producer). For radio, send the release to the show's host, producer, and news director.

13. Create and keep a database of media contacts. Send them news releases at least four times per year. Tie the release to a study, upcoming event (Christmas, graduation), something newsworthy. Check media websites or your local library for reference directories to local media. Call to verify names—people are constantly moving and changing jobs within stations or starting new shows and ending existing ones. Update your list regularly.

14. Consider writing several different versions of your news release, geared to different recipients. Targeted releases are the key to getting media attention for you or your business. For example, if you are announcing a festival that will feature Italian food, crafts, and entertainment, send one version to food magazines and food editors, with the emphasis on Italian food. Send another version emphasizing the entertain-

ment to the entertainment editors. Contacting multiple departments will increase the likelihood that you'll get coverage from someone at the newspaper or stations.

15. Keep press releases concise. No longer than one page. Never write a news release longer than two pages—no one will read it. Never fax a release that's longer than one page, because it's sure to get lost. TV stations and newspaper editors get hundreds of faxes each day, so make your release concise. Most large newspapers and TV and radio stations won't ever see a fax—to get your pitch in the appropriate person's hands, mail it directly to that person. It's worth mentioning that handwritten envelopes are opened faster than those with printed labels.

16. Write catchy headlines. The headline is the most important part of the news release, so it should be in type larger than the body copy (at least two to four points larger). The headline flags the editor to the importance of the news release, so if you are writing about an event that will occur on a certain date, it's a good idea to include the date in the headline.

17. Include statistics in your news releases whenever possible— they capture attention and add validity to the topic.

18. Never send photos or books that need to be returned— most reporters or producers are far too busy and, as standard operating procedure, do not return them.

19. Never follow up with a phone call asking, "Did you get my news release?" or, "Did you get my book?" or, "Do you know when it will be printed?" or, "Can you send me a copy once it's printed?" The media receive dozens of these annoying calls each day and don't have time to check. If you keep calling with these questions, you'll soon be branded as a pest. If you absolutely must follow up, a better approach is to call the person to whom you sent the release and ask if he or she needs additional information.

20. Don't waste money on ostentatious packaging for your news release, such as a release rolled up and tucked inside a gift box, then wrapped in plastic and tied with a big bow. News releases sent in packages that contain confetti or glitter are particularly annoying. The press will respond to headlines and releases that offer news and tips—concentrate on a news angle and skip the hype.

21. Tweak your press release and send it again. A new headline or angle might be all you need to get an editor or producer to call you. The angle is key. "News viewers, listeners, or readers can use" is the rationale the media applies in deciding what gets covered and what doesn't.

Free Up Time to Make More $$$

You need to be available and have time to do the things that generate income. Many businesses have failed because they remained too small. The perfect solution is to have one staff person—usually part-time. The person does the clerical stuff: answers phones, processes orders, does errands and word processing, responds to information requests, and so on. Getting help lets you accomplish more and generate more income by reducing the tasks that are time killers, not profit makers. This strategy is extremely effective in helping you avoid burnout—a prime consideration for business owners.

In some cases, the desire is simply to free up more time for your family, to go take a class, or for your own personal leisure. When you reach this stage, there are a few things you must consider about hiring staff. Staff can be a tremendous asset or a terrible liability. So be sure to follow these guidelines:

- **Delegate and train.** Create a training manual as you teach your assistants your office policies, procedures, and phone etiquette. Be sure they have written descriptions of your products and services, and then coach them on how to sell and talk to your clients. They need to secure business for you, not lose it, so teach them how. The training manual will be a good reference tool for them and for you, as it will be a big time-saver when you train new staff. Delineate duties and write a list of what you need your staff to accomplish on any given day, if it varies. Prioritize for them. Many staff people are not good at knowing what is most important. Left completely alone, they may do what they like and leave what they don't, so if time runs out, they don't have to do it.

Outline what you expect and state it. Be sure to share rules, office hours, paydays, sick leave, and so forth. A part-time staff person is of enormous benefit without the exorbitant costs that full-time help entails. If you are busy enough, then hire a full-time person. Be sure to clearly set up all office policies and learn about employee taxes from an accountant, so as not to get in trouble down the line.

- **_Hire the best you can find and pay above average._** Good assistants are worth every cent you pay them. Sometimes you want high school, minimum-wage help, and that's exactly what you'll get. That might work well for data processing and straight clerical tasks, but to build the business you'll also need someone who can represent and sell you to clients. I use both—a good assistant and a high schooler to occasionally do data entry or mailing projects for me.

  Good assistants are not hard to find or keep if you pay them well. Ask around your area—if the going part-time rate is $12 per hour, pay $13 or $14. You'll attract a better person, a true asset who'll make your business easier to run. You won't have to worry about losing him because he's underpaid. Staff turnover is a major hassle—a big time waster. Turnover also leads to lost revenues, so pay and train well, delegate tasks, and respect your staff. Your employees will stay for years to come. Be flexible and you'll increase your business's results and profits.

Strategies for Setting Business Fees and Prices for Products or Services

Nothing can seem more daunting than setting your fees. Many professional service companies fail to return each year and examine their costs and profit margins. The bottom line is not how much you earn, but how much you keep and how hard you work to make it in the first place.

You can reduce your workload by raising fees and doing more highly profitable things. Many small-business owners complain that although they become very successful, they aren't able to work less. Adding staff adds to overhead, and if revenues aren't skyrocketing, you often work harder and longer for only a little more take-home profit.

Let's take a few minutes to answer these questions about your business: What's the easiest thing you do to earn money? How many hours a day are you working at activities that pay you to do what you are doing? (Careful—answer this truthfully; only billable services or products count. Getting ready or marketing to get them does not.) How many hours are spent on nonbillable activities? What tasks can or should be delegated? What do competitors charge? Where's your niche? What is your most profitable product or service? What's your profit margin on each product and service?

Think bottom line—how much money you make doesn't matter, only how much you *keep*. Who are your best and most profitable clients? Is there an add-on business or service you can sell to your existing clients? How much of your time is spent on prospecting for new business? Nurturing current or old business? You need to really evaluate these questions. Give yourself several hours to track where the money goes and exactly where it comes from.

Your next step is to contain, or if possible cut, overhead ex-

Remember: 80% of your sales or income
comes from 20% of your clients.

penses. This will put more money in your pocket. Sometimes, by not actively monitoring costs, you can end up paying for services you don't need or want. It's better to buy good equipment that lasts and is problem-free than to buy inexpensive or bargain items that turn into headaches and eat your time fixing or hassling with them. Better equipment will always be a cost saver in the end. Also, beware of overkill. Four-color or metallic-embossed business cards may look cool, but the cost of printing them won't be. Pick good designs, logos, and marketing materials, and keep printing costs in mind when you make selections. Buy quality, but remember that two colors may be just as pleasing and less costly than four-color print jobs. One color is less expensive and can often be sufficient when paired with a nice design.

Next, review and outsource some tasks. For example, I keep a mailing list that's time-consuming to update. I wait until I have two or three hours of work, and then I hire the neighbor's high school–age son to enter the data into my system. I pay him half what I'd pay my assistant to do this. I also use this "cheaper labor" for mailing projects, filing, and putting together marketing packets and press kits—this saves me time and salary money.

Websites can be enormous time consumers. Design yours to be self-serving, with download features and recordable addresses for email newsletters. David, a one-person business owner, said, "I thought I didn't have the money to develop a great website, so I spent the time and learned the software and did it myself. My learning curve was over a hundred hours, and, yes, I can now add anything to it easily and personally. Looking back, I didn't get paid for any of the time I used doing it. Think how much income I lost, not working during those one hundred-plus hours.

I should have hired an outside resource and made money with my time. I'd be thousands of dollars ahead if I did. Learn from my mistake."

Some jobs require outside people. The cost of website development and updating it has decreased a great deal in the past few years. Hiring someone else for a flat fee to create your site, which allows you to work and make money, makes a great deal of economic sense. Review other areas of your business and outsource whenever possible so your time and attention can be spent on activities that you are being paid to do.

Our next step toward helping you generate more profitable income will be to conduct a survey of your competitors. This is an essential business step most owners do once in their start-up phase and forget to do again. Here are a few examples of how price surveys and adjustments helped business owners and professionals net (take home) more money.

Sue was a hairstylist who worked as an independent contractor. She talked with me when she wanted to move to a new salon. She followed my advice and surveyed her competitors; she found her fees were right in the middle pricewise. I advised her that relocating her business might cause her to lose some clientele and that she should keep the same fees with no increases for at least a year. Sue needed to retain people, and price increases would have added to the risk of losing clients when she moved to a new salon.

Since hers is a repeat business, she needed to retain as many clients as she could. She sent out a letter, map, and business card announcing her move to every old client she had. As a result, she kept 90% of her business. And as an added bonus, the mailing she sent to her entire client list (she never mailed to them before this) brought in some old customers who'd gone elsewhere. Her "recovery" of old, lost clients increased her revenues almost 20%. She made more than $100,000 that year and still averaged only thirty-five hours per week.

Tom was a CPA who owned his own practice and had developed a good clientele. He worked hard and had two full-time staff people, plus a part-time CPA who worked during tax season. Tom came to see me as a client when his wife became pregnant with their first child. They wanted her to quit her job and stay home with the baby but were concerned about losing her $40,000 annual income. Tom did the survey, as I suggested, and we evaluated his fees. I pointed out several things:

1. He greatly undervalued his services and had prices lower than those of most of his competitors.
2. He offered extra services to clients for free that other companies charged for.
3. He needed to generate a minimum of $100,000 in gross revenues to net $40,000 after expenses.

I warned Tom that his clients would be very upset and some would leave if he just doubled or tripled his prices. Instead, we created a menu of services and prices for each. He also offered a deluxe plan that lumped together many services. Tom sent all of his customers a letter explaining his "new" services—making recommendations for specific services that met client needs with listed rates. All rates went into effect sixty days after the letter went out.

Tom kept 70% of his clients but more than doubled his average bill. As a side benefit, his letter included a brochure with a handwritten note reading, "Pass this on to someone else I can help. Thanks, Tom." This generated several new (and higher-paying) clients. Much to Tom's surprise, it was his we-come-to-your-site computer training service that generated a great deal of revenue. He then put more effort into growing this highly profitable service, which resulted in his taking home twice what his wife used to make in extra income.

Bob, a graphic designer, wanted only high-end clientele. His prices were high, set to his target market of big, high-paying corporations. His quality was fresh and innovative. He said one reason for the higher price was that big corporations often take three to four months to pay their bills—they can afford and expect high fees. This is how he justified bigger price tags, because he wanted fewer clients and big-name projects. His challenge was to deliver everything the client wanted, though he was only a small, two-man shop. For years he averaged one hundred hours a week and made excellent money working for a few household-name clients. Then two major things impacted him in the same twelve months. Three clients merged, and with each merger he lost their business. "I got left out in the cold," he said. Then he went through a bitter divorce. He kept his business going, but he had no energy to go after new business to replace the old. Split custody forced him to work less. His problems eventually drove him to simply want to close his business. We worked together, and he found a good job as director of marketing at a Fortune 500 company—a move he said was a great solution. Now his career and his life is flourishing again.

The moral of the story is this: You must always be prospecting for new clients and customers. Coasting or resting on your laurels, so to speak, can and will come back and bite you. That said, folks, life happens. If you go through enough personal crises—divorce, pregnancy, illness, sick parents or child—your business *will* suffer. You'll be too consumed to care until you are forced to. Plan for a rainy day. *Save* no less than three months of overhead in an account to cover the business losses that can occur when a great client goes bankrupt or your personal life takes a big dive. Hire extra help during long-term situations, such as when you or your parents are sick, to cover duties you can't or just don't want to do!

Now it's time to examine your pricing structure. Fill out this cost sheet and competitor survey.

Profit per Item List each product, one per line	YOUR PRODUCTS		
	Retail Cost	Your Cost	Profit per Item

You may not know exactly how much your competitors pay for their products, but do try to find out by calling them or visiting their websites. Note several competitors and all their services that you offer (it's also smart to list any services they offer that you don't but could potentially add).

The next step to setting competitive fees is to analyze the true costs of your products. The true product cost is: Marketing Fee + Overhead Fee + Product Expense = True Cost of Product − Your Cost to Obtain. Here's how to compute and figure out each of these costs. To determine your monthly overhead cost, take your set annual expenses—annual rent, phones, staff, supplies, postage, and so on—for last year and divide that number by twelve. This is your current monthly total. For our example, let's use the case of Sarah, a client I helped. She was a national trainer, and her overhead ran $84,000 per year, making her monthly costs $7,000. The next step is to divide the monthly cost by the number of products, programs, or services sold in a month—say, ten programs. So $7,000 in overhead costs, divided by ten programs sold, equals $700 for an overhead expense per product. Now, total her yearly marketing costs—brochures, ads, staff time, packets, postage, videos, cards, and so on. Let's say it was $12,000 per year, or $1,000 per month. Divide $1,000 by the average monthly number of programs (which is ten). This comes out to $100. Therefore, the marketing cost is $100 per program.

Okay, let's put it together to see how we add the overhead, product, and marketing costs to correctly set training program fees. Assuming all travel expenses are covered by the client, our trainer's program costs are $100 for marketing and training materials, plus $700 for overhead, equaling $800 in costs. Therefore, if she's charging $1,000 per program, her true net is only $200, not $1,000. This is a key concept many people miss. You must add in overhead and marketing costs to determine the true cost of your products or services sold.

Sarah needs to charge no less than $800 just to meet her costs. Likewise, she needs to assess the value of the program she delivers to clients. To set a price, I recommend tripling the cost.

Why? Tripling (or charging a higher fee) usually reduces the number of customers and the owners' workload while increasing revenues and overall profits. Look closely at the difference in rates if Sarah doubles or triples her program fee. By doubling her fee and charging $1,600, she likely will sell and do more programs. She'll work more, thus working harder to earn her take-home pay. To work less and make more, she needs to increase her fee more substantially. With her extra time she can provide more personal service to her clients or perhaps develop a consulting business to generate even more profitable income.

ANNUAL PROJECT FEES

	Number of Programs	Price	Overhead Costs	Annual Net Profit
Charging fees— doubled	100	$160,000	$80,000	$80,000
Charging fees— tripled	75	$160,000	$60,000	$120,000
Charging fees— tripled	50	$120,000	$40,000	$80,000

Use Sarah's example in the table shown. List your own current fees and costs, then projected doubled fees and projected tripled fees. Realize that by raising fees significantly, you'll lose some customers. Note that Sarah projects 25% fewer training programs if she triples her costs. Notice that when she charges $2,400, she has to do only fifty programs, at a profit of $1,600 each, to net $80,000 in take-home income (before taxes). This is what she makes by doing twice as many programs—one hundred programs—if she only doubles her fees. If she triples her fees and does seventy-five programs, she'll net $120,000—less work than one hundred programs and a great deal more profit. That's the key to moving your business up. Charge enough to be very well paid for your time. Don't just get a ton of work and become totally exhausted completing it because your fees are too low. Undercutting your prices only hurts you. If you suffer from a "poverty complex" about changing fees, that's something you must get over.

Alan Weiss, author of *Million Dollar Consulting* (McGraw-Hill, 1998), said, "Most consultants undercharge and overdeliver because they don't place significant value on themselves. They just don't recognize their true worth or value—they suffer from low self-esteem and lack of confidence in themselves and, as a result, make less money. Women are worse than men. Women have natural attributes essential to being a good consultant, such as good listening skills, but they have much lower estimates of their marketplace value, so due to low confidence they usually earn significantly less than their male counterparts. You need to charge fees based on the value your client or customer receives from what you sell."

When you set your prices for selling any service or product, always add in the overhead and marketing costs. For example, you might sell videos for \$20. Your costs are \$8 for duplication and a jacket, plus \$2 for overhead and \$1 for marketing, equaling \$11 in costs. Your profit would be \$9 per video, but only if you incurred no other costs to distribute it—for example, if you paid staff to ship or mail it. You'll likely need to add \$.50 or \$1.00 for processing time and staff salary costs. That gives you a product with a true cost of about \$11.50. Now, set your retail price so you aren't overestimating your profit. Subtracting operating expenses must be a part of setting prices for every product or service you sell.

Summary of Setting Your Pricing Fees

Rule 1 Know what your competitor charges.
Rule 2 Frequent price increases are noticed and annoy your customers. Therefore, set prices you can live with for two years or more.
Rule 3 Get paid the maximum dollar for the time worked.
Rule 4 Eliminate tasks that require too much of your unpaid time by either delegating or deleting them altogether.
Rule 5 Give customers more than what they expect or paid for in the service or product.

Learn Business Skills from Business Experts

We all have the same number of hours in any given day. How you manage and use your time is what will impact your results. If you haven't done so, invest in a time management seminar. I think Franklin Covey's (800-901-1776) full-day program teaches some practical and useful tips.

I recommend learning from experts. This allows you to glean the best knowledge necessary to be more profitable in your business. Any small business will fail if the owner does not possess good marketing and accounting skills.

Marketing is key to acquiring clients or customers. Sales mean closing deals and getting people to bring you money. There are three ways to acquire marketing and sales skills: read books, take classes, or hire a consultant or coach.

Some things can be learned from books, like public relations, writing press releases, creating ad copy, setting up a database, and so on. Coaches and classes are more expensive, but effective. To learn about direct mail, you could take a seminar sponsored by the Direct Mail Association. If you'd rather learn at home, a tape series is worth the investment of time and money. David Garfinkel offers a thorough tape series program with a workbook entitled *The Money Making Copying Writing Course,* avalable at www.killercopytactics.com. Every entrepreneur can benefit from writing better marketing and sales copy.

Maybe you'd like to have a product or two but aren't ready to write a book. I think Paulette Ensign's program is a valuable resource for learning how to write, produce, and sell informational booklets. She'll give you a lot of usable information for your buck in her tape series programs, *How to Write and Market Booklets for Ca$h* and *How to Promote Your Business with Booklets.* Both are available at www.tipsbooklets.com.

Many people like to learn HTML or other Web programs to handle their website designs and updates. I personally find this task so time-consuming that I outsource it, hiring a consultant to do it for me. Outsource when you need to and use your time doing what makes you money.

Sometimes buying help leads to years of rewards. Hiring a copywriter or graphic designer to create or improve your brochure will continually earn you customers and dollars long after they're gone and their bills are paid.

There is one thing you must do personally, and that is learn accounting principles. You must understand overhead costs, profit ratios, taxes, budgeting, and so forth. Many community colleges offer programs for small-business owners—take one and set up a good accounting and bookkeeping system that's easy to use and gives feedback on sales vs. expenses. You should hire an accountant to handle tax functions, but you must be aware and knowledgeable about operating expenses and gross vs. net income to increase profitability.

Professional associations and colleges can be great sources of business skills training programs. Attending seminars and workshops offered by top experts can be very worthwhile investment. Every business owner needs to learn terrific business operations and management skills. In fact, most successful doctors, lawyers, accountants, and consultants weren't simply born with good business operation skills. They learned and perfected these skills by investing thousands of dollars in continuing education, practice management courses, and special training programs.

Summary

The sky's the limit when you own your own business. The thrills of success, plus the hours and hard work, can enrich your life or destroy it. Only you can decide what you want. Trim and cut costs as needed, but create a company where you want to go to work every day. Some working parents will create a business that gives them freedom, flexibility, and more family time. Others will push ahead and get bigger. It's all up to you. Decide, plan, and go for it!

> The good news is it doesn't take as much to stay at the top as it does to get there. Maybe we just get better at juggling it all. Anyway, it sure is worth it.
> —Sunny Kobe Cooke, founder of
> Sleep Country USA, national retail chain

PART 4

Conclusion
Go for It!

The difference between a successful person and others is not a lack of strength, not a lack of knowledge, but rather in a lack of will.

—VINCE LOMBARDI, LEGENDARY NFL COACH

CHAPTER 10

The Rewards of Meaningful Work

A few times in your life you dream something
so big, so outrageous, it seems a fantasy. But
then, as you move on with your dream, you
forge a path. A hope. A desire. A want. A goal.

Those incredible fantasies become less
outrageous and actually probable. Somewhere
along the way you realize you *can* do it. You *can*.
You *will*. You *must*. Your happiness depends on
it. Settle for nothing less than your best. You'll
be amazed at what you can accomplish when
you try hard enough.

—RR

Your goals and deepest desires do matter. The value and reward
of performing passionate, meaningful work is that it fulfills our
dreams, motivates, and enriches us. The greatest career advice I
can offer is really a gift you must give yourself—a career, job, or
business you are passionate about. With typical workers putting
in eleven thousand workdays over their lifetimes, nothing will

improve your life like having a job you love. This book is dedicated to just that goal—profiting from work you enjoy.

Truth be told, it's rarely money that motivates. I left a prestigious university position as director of counseling services because I didn't like the job. I then opened my own career counseling and seminar business, working harder than ever, clocking eighty-hour work weeks to make a go of my business. Many people warned me: "No one is making it in the career business." But my motivation was simple—to help people find jobs and more personal satisfaction from their careers. It's what I love to do—it's rewarding and fulfilling, and I've achieved success beyond my wildest dreams. Three years ago, at age forty-two, I had a baby, and as a result, I made a career change and cut my hours to no more than thirty per week. I now focus on writing, coaching clients, and giving some speeches. I have eliminated a great deal in order to blend my professional passion with my desire to be active in raising my son, Jack.

I still love my job—I literally couldn't live without it. Yet I love being with Jack as my little four-year-old explores the world. I shared his first words, steps, and smiles. I snap pictures almost daily—these happy family memories are recorded on film as well as in my heart. What makes me whole is having time for both my family and work. I'm living the life I want to live.

You, too, can reinvent your life and your career, achieving whatever your heart desires. It's never too late to follow your dreams. So many of my clients have done just that and now find they love their jobs and their lives. For Michelle Townsend, the path was roundabout. In high school, she loved building things and had a natural talent for it. Encouraged to train for a more practical career because she was a woman, she went into retail work after college and excelled as a buyer. But her passion for building did not diminish, so in her early thirties, while working full-time, Michelle began the long process of going back to college for a degree in construction management. Upon graduation, she left the department store and followed her dream, taking a pay cut in the process. But Michelle fast-tracked, drawing on her previous management skills, is now a project manager for a large national commercial construction company, and is "loving every minute of it," she told me.

Daniel worked for years as a marketing manager. But in his spare time, he volunteered for environmental causes—he was an advocate for political change. He raised four kids and, at forty-eight years old, decided to pursue his *true* dream—to become a lawyer so he could really influence environmental changes. Today he's a lobbyist, using his law degree to help create new legislation protecting the environment he loves so much.

Another client, Andy, had a passion—he loved to fly airplanes and show people the wonders above the ground. When he lost his sales job with a major airplane maker after a reorganization, he was devastated. The derailment was tough—he feared he'd never, *ever*, find that kind of job again. At fifty, Andy felt the "good life" was over. He avoided airports at all costs; it was just too painful.

Then he got wind of a new plane being designed by a prominent airplane maker, and that led to his uncovering a potential sales job. He applied. After the initial interview, he was invited to corporate headquarters for a couple of days of testing and interviews. An hour before he was to leave for the airport, his father-in-law died. When Andy called the company, they told him they had hired a consultant to do an "evaluation" and that he needed to come within two days to be considered. He went. They gave him a videotaped test of an angry customer and another of a disgruntled employee—both went well. The third part was the "inbox test"—a stack of memos and notes to deal with. After completing the test, Andy had a feeling it didn't go well and returned home to wait for the results.

He finally got a call from John, the company manager. It seemed Andy flunked the "in-box test"—the results said he was disorganized. But Andy did not take that failure for a "no" answer. He sat down and composed a well-crafted two-page letter to persuade John, the hiring manager, that not only was he well organized, but he was a good salesman, too. John later commented on one line that read, "I'm not used to flunking tests! I have had success at everything from carrier landings to getting an MBA." Andy then quoted his sales record and painted a detailed picture of *how* organized he is in his home office, with "A," "B," and "C" in-boxes. He told John about the numerous computerized programs he used to track and keep up with the hundreds of clients he had at his old job. The employer was convinced. "I got it!" Andy called me to say. "This job is a dream come true! To most people, it looks like another sales position with another big company! But to me, it's perfect. I beat out two thousand applicants—thirty of whom made it to the interview stage—now I'm their regional sales manager. If you're a pilot like I am, and you love flying more than anything else, there are only a handful of jobs selling pleasure planes in America. Now, one of them is mine!"

Many people find excuses for not making their dreams come true. Not so with Stina Cowan, who moved to Seattle from Sweden. Formerly a teacher in Brussels for a Swedish school, Cowan was disappointed that Seattle had no such school here, so she started one. Just six months later, twenty-four kids were attending the new school for two hours of weekly instruction in Swedish language, history, geography, and culture, with all classes taught in Swedish. Now, as director of that school, she keeps her culture alive for her own two kids and sixty other Swedish children.

Getting a new business off the ground requires a passion that drives you. A conviction and attitude to succeed are essential. You need to seek out advice, conduct market research, plan well, and learn from your mistakes, for everyone makes many when they start out. But what else is required, once you are successful, to take "your baby" to the next level? "Be careful what you dream about," warned Robin Wes, "as dreams have a way of coming true." Wes's dream began twenty-four years ago, when he was a physical education teacher with a love of music. People told him he was crazy when he talked about a place where toddlers, preschoolers, and elementary school children could go for physical education classes taught cleverly with music. "I had no doubt in my mind that I'd succeed," Wes said. "When you have a strong vision to propel you, well, that's how people reach goals."

Wes's business, the Little Gym, did well. Small classes, enjoyable programs, and happy customers were the keys to its success. After a few years, Wes's dream began to change. He started thinking about seeing Little Gyms all over the country. Wes explored franchising, sought legal advice, and conducted market research. After seven years of planning, he successfully launched the franchising of his Little Gyms. Thousands of young children every day are now entertained and exercised at Little Gym franchises. Wes says that while planning is very important, people who offer quality programs and good customer service seldom fail. Wes has done what most businesses owners salivate over— he took his small business and franchised it. Today there are more than one hundred Little Gyms in the United States, with several more in Europe and Asia.

Although success is sweet and, as in Wes's case, often financially rewarding, there's more to career dreams than just money and success. When Stina Cowan stands up in front of her Swedish class and talks about her homeland, the gleam in her eye comes from teaching American kids about a country she loves. And at the Little Gym near my home in Seattle, you can still find Robin Wes leading a class for babies and parents. (If you'd stopped by on a Thursday morning last year, you would have also found me—taking time from my workday—to dance around with my toddler, Jack.) No matter how big the Little Gyms have become, Wes still finds pleasure in picking up his guitar, smiling brightly into those tiny faces, and singing his heart out.

It's passion that makes the difference. Your dreams and deepest desires do matter, so select work you can fall in love with.

Then go a step further and be sure that it's allowing you to live
the life you want and not causing you to miss the family experiences that enrich us all. It's the key to your long-term happiness.

That's what I want for you—that you'll experience that feeling of fulfillment every day you go to work. I wrote this book to
guide you in making a career change that will enrich your life
and give you all the things you're longing for. I've given you the
tools, action steps, and expert advice to help you. Now it's your
turn to enact your plan and make it happen.

So here's my final recommendation for you:

> Act as if it were impossible to fail,
> and you never will.
>
> —ROBIN RYAN

More Career Help Available

Robin Ryan has written other valuable career materials that are excellent resources to aid you in your career change. Her books and audiotapes, available in bookstores and from her website www.robinryan.com include these:

60 Seconds & You're Hired! (covers interviewing and salary
  negotiations)
Winning Resumés
Winning Cover Letters
The Power of Branding You audiotape series

She offers career counseling, resumé writing services, interview coaching, and assistance with salary negotiations via telephone consultations. For corporate clients she provides outplacement, spouse relocation, and executive coaching services.

A popular national speaker, having presented over 1,200 speeches, Robin is available to speak to your group, company, or organization.

Visit her website for more details about her speaking and career coaching services.

You can also sign up for her email newsletter, *Career News You Can Use,* at her website, www.robinryan.com.

To contact Robin Ryan, call her Seattle office at (425) 226-0414. E-mail her at robinryan@aol.com, or visit her website at www.robinryan.com.

Recommended Resources

Books

Richard Bayan, *Words That Sell: A Thesaurus to Help Promote Your Products, Services, and Ideas* (Chicago: Contemporary Books Inc., 1984). A terrific must-own resource for business owners.

Marcus Buckingham and Curt Coffman, *First Break All the Rules: What the World's Greatest Managers Do Differently* (New York: Simon & Schuster, 1999). A must read with groundbreaking research on rising to the top.

Jack Canfield and Mark Victor Hansen, *Dare to Win* (New York: Berkley Publishing Group, 1996). A good motivational book on thinking, believing, and achieving.

Sunny Kobe Cook, *Common Things, Uncommon Ways* (Seattle: Achievement Dynamics, 2002). This author built a $350 million company perfecting the art of developing staff. Every manager and business owner should read and use her ideas.

Paul and Sarah Edwards, *Working from Home: Everything You Need to Know About Living and Working Under the Same Roof,* 5th rev. ed. (New York: Jeremy P. Tarcher, 1999). These authors are authorities on the home-based business world. I've found all of their books to be terrific resources.

Jeffrey J. Fox, *How to Become CEO: The Rules for Rising to the Top of Any Organization* (New York: Hyperion, 1998). This gem has brief chapters and great ideas for those up for the move to the top.

Azriela Jaffe, *Create Your Own Luck: 8 Principles of Attracting Good Fortune in Life, Love, and Work* (Holbrook, Mass.: Adams Media Corp., 2000). Jaffe shows how resourceful people make their own luck using solid strategies—an inspiring, useful book. I highly recommend it.

———, *Honey, I Want to Start My Own Business: A Planning Guide for Couples* (New York: HarperCollins, 1996). Designed to guide the would-be small-business owner, this book has great insights, tools, and self-assessment exercises for making a go of business ownership.

Robert E. Kelley, *How to Be a Star at Work: 9 Breakthrough Strategies You Need to Succeed* (New York: Random House, 1998). New research with specific ideas for moving ahead.

Cynthia Kersey, *Unstoppable: 45 Powerful Stories of Perseverance and Triumph from People Just Like You* (Naperville, Ill.: Sourcebooks, 1998). An inspiring book for added motivation.

Philip Lief Group and Lynie Arden, *220 Best Franchises to Buy* (New York: Broadway Books, 2000). Good overview on costs, start-up needs, and business outlook projections.

Terri Lonier, *Working Solo: The Real Guide to Freedom and Financial Success with Your Own Business,* 2nd ed. (New York: John Wiley & Sons, 1998). This author is the guru in this area and has a whole series of resources to help those who want the freedom and flexibility to work for themselves.

Miriam Otte, *Marketing with Speeches and Seminars: Your Key to More Clients and Referrals* (Seattle, Wash.: Zest Press, 1998). Excellent overview for using speeches to build a business and get more clients or customers.

Raleigh Pinskey, *101 Ways to Promote Yourself* (New York: Avon Books, 1997). A gold mine of ideas to make your business more successful.

Eileen Roth, with Elizabeth Miles, *Organizing for Dummies* (Foster City, Calif.: IDG Books Worldwide, 2001). Better than the rest—useful and practical.

Robin Ryan, *Winning Resumés* (New York: John Wiley & Sons, 2002). Provides employer survey on the best way to write a resumé using an easy, effective seven-step method.

———, *Winning Cover Letters* (New York: John Wiley & Sons, 2002). Employer survey outlines key mistakes to avoid. Also offers successful letter samples for targeting the hidden job market.

———, *60 Seconds & You're Hired!* (New York: Penguin, 2000). Your guide to interview success and salary negotiations. Teaches you how to develop and use the 60 Second Sell, a proven tool to use during interviews to land a job.

Alexandra Stoddard, *The Art of the Possible: The Path from Perfectionism to*

Balance and Freedom (New York: Avon Books, 1995). A warm look at achieving a purposeful life. I've always enjoyed this author's books—this one is a good supplement, one that women in particular will enjoy.

Brian Tracy, *Focal Point: A Proven System to Simplify Your Life, Double Your Productivity, and Achieve All Your Goals* (New York: AMACOM, 2001). A terrific book on setting and accomplishing goals.

Alan Weiss, *Getting Started in Consulting* (New York: John Wiley & Sons, 2000). A must-own resource if you want to delve into the consulting business.

———, *Million Dollar Consulting: The Professional's Guide to Growing a Practice* (New York: McGraw-Hill, 1997). A good book for developing, organizing, and promoting a highly profitable consulting business.

Audiocassettes

Paulette Ensign, *How to Promote Your Business with Booklets* (program with audiotapes and manual) (San Diego, Calif.: Tips Products International), www.tipsbooklets.com.

———, *How to Write and Market Booklets for Ca$h* (program with videotape and manuals) (San Diego, Calif.: Tips Products International). Ensign's easy-to-follow programs explain how small-business owners can sell more products and services and gain new clients by producing promotional booklets.

Earl Nightingale, *The Essence of Success* (Nightingale-Conant Corp., 1991). I have this series and listen to it often. It is excellent and should be used over and over again.

Nightingale-Conant, 1-800-323-5552 or www.nightingale.com. Check out their catalog and Web site for many excellent tapes on success and achievement.

Brian Tracy, *How to Master Your Time* (Nightingale-Conant Corp., 1989). Good ideas and philosophy that work to make you more productive.

Associations

Alumni associations. Career counseling is available for alumni through many colleges and universities. Contact your institution to find out what services are available.

Small Business Administration—www.sba.gov.

6 **Recommended Resources**

Websites

www.robinryan.com. Numerous career and job search articles available. Also, subscribe to e-newsletter *Career News You Can Use*.

www.workingfromhome.com. This excellent site is run by Paul and Sarah Edwards, authorities on the home-based business world.

Inc.com. *Inc.* magazine's site is full of useful information.

www.websitessuccess.net. Good ideas for creating profitable and popular Web sites.

www.publicityhound.com. Information on publicity.

www.nsaspeaker.com. A good resource for learning how to market your speeches.

Other

QuickBooks. Good accounting software program.

Toastmasters. Public speaking organization—best way to improve or learn skills.

About the Author

One of the nation's foremost career authorities, ROBIN RYAN is the best-selling author of six books—including *60 Seconds & You're Hired!*, *Winning Resumés*, and *Winning Cover Letters*—and creator of the audiotape series *The Power of Branding You*. Robin Ryan has appeared on more than seven hundred TV and radio programs, including *NBC Nightly News with Tom Brokaw, Oprah, CNN,* and *CNBC,* and appears regularly on Bloomberg Radio, Seattle's KOMO Radio and TV plus Fox TV's *Mornings Live* show. A consistent contributor to national magazines and trade publications, she's been featured in *Money, Newsweek, Fortune, Business Week, Cosmopolitan, Glamour* and *McCall's,* to name a few. She's appeared on the pages of most major newspapers, including *USA Today, The Wall Street Journal, The New York Times, the Los Angeles Times,* the *Boston Herald,* and the *Chicago Tribune.* She has been a *Seattle Times* career columnist for six years.

A licensed vocational counselor for twenty years, Robin Ryan has an active career counseling practice based in Seattle, where she offers telephone consultations and assists clients with career changing, resumés, job search, interviewing, salary negotiation, and other career issues. Additionally, her work includes outplacement consulting and executive coaching. She holds a master's degree in counseling and education from Suffolk University and a bachelor's degree in sociology from Boston College and is the former director of counseling services at the University of Washington. A popular national speaker, Robin Ryan has conducted over 1,200 seminars and keynote programs, contributing to the career success of millions of people.

You can contact Robin Ryan at 425-226-0414.
Website: www.robinryan.com